Willy Victor and 25 Knot Hole

Willy Victor and 25 Knot Hole

Bruce Jarvis

Library of Congress Control Number:		2012916565
ISBN:	Hardcover	978-1-4797-1367-7
	Softcover	978-1-4797-1366-0
	Ebook	978-1-4797-1368-4

This book was printed in the United States of America.

This book is edited by: Ms. Christine Hawver

To order additional copies of this book, contact:
Xlibris Corporation
1-888-795-4274
www.Xlibris.com
Orders@Xlibris.com
121360

Table of Contents

To my wife Mary whose love and support
motivated me to continue this effort

Preface

My interest in writing this story was inspired by the Honorable Tim Johnson, an Illinois Congressman. He gave a speech at a Willy Victor flyers reunion at Chanute, AFB in 2003. He told the audience that until he was asked to speak at the reunion, he had no knowledge of what the group of people he was speaking to did for their country during the cold war. The Congressman indicated that he was overwhelmed with their mission achievements. He indicated that 99.99% of the United States public had no idea what was done or accomplished. His message motivated me to share my story with the public. Following the reunion, it took me three years to get started on this story. Just finding a way to begin was difficult as it had been about 45 years since I had left the Navy for civilian life. Once I started remembering what I and many others experienced, I continued writing until the story was finished. The stories all are true with a little bit of fiction weaved throughout.

During 1946, Winston Churchill contacted President Harry Truman to provide him with his thoughts about Russia's intentions to drape an Iron Curtain over Eastern Europe. Shortly thereafter the Russians began the blockade of Berlin. Following the blockade they took over the countries of Poland, Czechoslovakia, and Ukraine. This time is thought to be the beginning of the Cold War between the Free and Communist worlds.

In the early hours of April 17, 1952 World War III nearly began. The previous afternoon an intelligence source had reported unusual levels of activity at Soviet airbases. Shortly after midnight United States Air Defense Command in Colorado Springs, got word from Alaska that vapor trails from bogeys had been sighted high over the Bering Sea, coming from the direction of the Soviet Union. As Generals fretted over the report, another message arrived. Five more aircraft had been sighted off the coast of Maine. It might have been the real thing. The paranoia of the Cold War may be coming true, in a sneak atomic attack. Hence, the Generals ordered a full alert. Fighters were scrambled; Bombers were prepared and taxied to the end of the runways at many bases to fly a retaliatory strike.

What was the end result of all of this activity? Nothing! The vapor trails disappeared; the unknowns over Maine were identified as airliners off course. The perceived threat vanished. Most of the people in the United States slept that night undisturbed. But, the North American Defense Command (NORAD) had acted without real evidence of an attack. The biggest issue was the length of time it took for the first report of enemy planes to get to Colorado Springs and even longer for NORAD to finally figure out what was going on: ninety minutes. The methods to identify enemy aircraft were outdated. Hence, the Distance Early Warning Line (DEW) was developed, built, and went operational in 1957.

But, unfortunately the DEW line's radar coverage did not initially provide any defense whatsoever against aircraft approaching the United States coasts from the northwest and northeast over the ocean approaches. The ocean approaches were longer however, the Soviets were already flying aircraft prototypes of turboprop bombers with the range to fly just such missions. Adjuncts to the DEW line electronic radar barriers were needed to patrol off shore on both coasts to prevent long range aircraft from penetrating air defenses and reaching the continental United States without warning.

I am writing a portion of this story to describe the Airborne Early Warning Squadrons (AEWRON) mission and the people and aircraft that accomplished it. It was these squadrons that were designated and their operations implemented to cover the Atlantic and Pacific Ocean approaches. They were the extensions of the DEW line. The AEWRON's flew their missions over the Atlantic and Pacific Oceans from 1956-1967. The routes they flew were called barriers. Airborne early warning flights continued during the Viet Nam war to protect the Pacific Fleet sailing in those waters in and around Viet Nam. The barrier missions were stood down as Satellites took them over in 1968.

The time frame for my story is 1956-1959. The story is about my experiences while serving in the United States Navy during this portion of the Cold War. It began in early 1956 at Great Lakes Illinois and ended at the Brooklyn Navy Yard in August 1959. From September 1957 until early August 1959 I spent flying the Atlantic Barrier as a member of flight crews 5 and 11 knothole in Air Early Warning Squadron (AEWRON)-11 or VW-11.

"25 knothole" is a fictional crew of sailors who are a combination of real and fictional people who lived the mission day to day. The stories are real, lived by the crew and their squadron. The aircraft used to fly the barrier was the Lockheed Super Constellation Morning Star. (Willy Victor-2, Navy designation) The crew of "25 knothole" was members of VW-11. It is one crew among many with the thousands of Sailors and Air Force personnel that supported the missions. Our story includes the purpose of the missions, their importance, the people who flew them, some of their stories, personnel that supported them, their families, their women, their wives, their frustrations, their happy moments and their sad.

Why did I pick VW-11 as the Squadron for the story? I was a member of VW-11 and spent two years flying the Atlantic barrier. Who am I? I started out as a seventeen year old who had no idea what he had begun when his dad agreed to sign the enlistment papers for him. I ended up participating in an adventure that protected my country and completely changed my life.

There were many of us flying out of Newfoundland, Hawaii, Guam, and from Air Force bases up and down the East and West coasts of the United States. Some locations were more desirable to be stationed at than others, but all had the same mission, flying barriers, identifying bogies, and reporting them to the North American Air Defense Command (NORAD). It was then up to NORAD to determine who, what, when, and why an aircraft was flying where it was, who and what it was, and whether or not it was to be shot down. I would have liked to include the details of this information but, all of the contact data and the data from NORAD remains classified today and is unavailable for this effort.

There are no monuments for those who gave their lives flying and training in the Willy Victor and EC-121 aircraft. This aircraft was developed to fly the various barriers around the world protecting the United States of America and the free world from its enemies during this dangerous time in the Cold War. Mr. Donald J. "DJ" Dunnarumma began the story and Mr. Wes Mortenson continued the process with the web page Willy Victor.com. As of the writing of this story both Messers. Dunnarumma and Mortenson have passed on to greater glory. Hopefully my contribution will continue their efforts and be an additional vehicle that memorializes those who made the ultimate sacrifice for our country, those of us that survived the barriers and those who maintained the aircraft they flew in. In fact, since we actually didn't fight in wars in a foreign country during this time frame, 1956-59, we are not eligible to join the VFW.

Chapter 1

Distant Early Warning Line
(DEW line)

There was a panic at the North American Defense Command (NORAD) in early 1952. Aircraft were intruding into Canadian Air space from over the North Pole, but notification at NORAD wasn't received until three weeks after it happened. Following that situation, at the Air Force behest a gathering of eminent scientists and engineers called the Lincoln Summer Study Group met at Lincoln Laboratories during the summer of 1952. The purpose of this group was to study the United States air defense issues. Among the conferees were J. Robert Oppenheimer and I.I. Rabi (both veterans of the Manhattan project). These were men accustomed to thinking large and solving problems associated with them.

Prior to 1952 the United States had begun to improve its air defense effort. A post war radar network called Lashup, deployed around some major cities, was being beefed up and two radar fences were under construction: The Pine Tree line, along the U.S.-Canadian border and the unstaffed Mid-Canada line further north near the fifty-fifth parallel. They were useful against slow-moving propeller-driven planes but, totally inadequate for the jet age. The Lincoln Group pointed out that by the time Soviet jets crossed these thresholds, it would be too late to stop them. Only by detecting intruders earlier could an attack be thwarted.

The Lincoln group also knew that the shortest route for Soviet bombers approaching the United States would be across the North Pole. Such an attack could be detected only by constructing radar stations in the far north, stretching across the top of the Western hemisphere inside the Arctic Circle from Alaska to Greenland, covering the entire airspace and connected to the United States by reliable communications. Such a network could provide up to four hours' warning to prepare defenses and hopefully evacuate at least some of the populace from target cities. In December 1952 in one of his last acts before leaving the presidency, Harry S. Truman approved the concept.

Over the next year it was debated by the military and civilian alike. Cost was one issue. Projected to be over hundreds of millions, some doubted the scheme would work, or that it could prevent nuclear war. Still others thinking back a dozen years to France in World War II, feared a "Maginot Line mentality", in which a defensive barrier would yield a false sense of impregnability. In the end, whatever its imperfections, the benefits of such a radar fence made it indispensable as part of the revamped air-defense system, which would also include improved surveillance on the ground and in the air, advance communications, computing facilities, and a centralized staff to put all of the information together. It was an elegant and simple idea.

In practice it would be an entirely different matter. The problems were daunting. How to get all the equipment up there? What about communications in the unreliable atmospheric conditions of the far north, with its magnetic and electrical anomalies? How well would our radars work? How could we build permanent structures in Arctic conditions? To find out the Defense Department hired Western Electric Corporation, a massive subsidiary of ATT, to build several experimental stations, one in rural Illinois and several in Alaska for testing. The success of the tests and the first thermonuclear explosion by the Soviets in 1953 convinced the military that the Defense Early Warning Line (DEW line) was feasible and necessary. Politics was not the issue. The Canadian government gave permission to the U.S. to build the stations as long as the U.S. footed the bill. In December 1954 Western Electric was awarded the contract with the stipulation that the DEW line was to be completed and operational by July 31, 1957.

The enormity and difficulty of the task can only be described as horrific. The sites were built roughly along the 69th parallel, on land that was uninhabited, with the exception of widely scattered outposts of nomadic Inuit natives. Temperatures would drop as low as 60 degrees below zero F with 100 mph winds that would freeze flesh in seconds. For three months of the year the sun never rises above the horizon. Sites were picked using small planes and had to be void of mountains so they wouldn't interfere with radar, communications or access by air. Ideally the sites would have sea access. Sixty sites were determined to meet the criteria. Airstrips had to be built at each site to provide access for supplies for construction teams and operating teams. The delivery of initial supplies and personnel amounted to the largest commercial airlift ever assembled. Almost 150,000 tons of supplies were carried in 45,000 flights using hundreds of aircraft. Twenty five men died in air crashes the first year. During the 3 years of construction when the frozen Arctic began melting in the summer, some 120 ships brought 42,000 tons of steel, millions of gallons of fuel, and many other supplies. On July 31, 1957 a miracle job completed, Western Electric turned over to the Air Force the fully operational DEW line. A complete 62 operating stations strung out over 3000 miles.

The DEW line operated with modifications and changes until 1990 when the United States turned over its operation to Canada. It seems to have done its job. No one attacked the United States or Canada during the Cold War. In the eyes of the veterans, both civilian and military, it did its job. The cooperation of the military, industry, Inuits, United States and Canadian peoples made this endeavor successful. It was one of the efforts that led to the good guys winning the Cold War.

The early planning envisioned a need for augmenting the basic radar net, because it would not give any real warning of enemy aircraft approaching from the east or west via the Atlantic and Pacific Oceans toward the American coastlines. Thus, the original thinking called for two lines of warning, called barriers, to be set up off shore of the two coasts. Each barrier would be made up of a number of stations and aircraft at each station would orbit in a long racetrack pattern. Initial Air Force thinking in 1951 provided 56 AEW&C aircraft flying 800 mile barriers located 224 miles off shore with aircraft flying on station some 150 miles apart. In effect there would be an electronic wall 800 miles long and 0-40,000 feet high. This concept was refined to extend the barrier further from the continental coasts when the Soviets exploded a thermonuclear device in August 1953.

The next step was to determine who would implement the idea. At this time a rivalry began between the Air Force and the Navy concerning the proposed new radar picket operations. The Air Force had the primary responsibility for continental air defense, including the DEW line. The Navy's only clear responsibility at that time was providing a few radar picket ships which would patrol off-shore and with their radar pinpoint enemy aircraft trying to sneak in at very low altitudes. The Air Force felt it had the responsibility for the off shore airborne radar picket operations, but, the Navy happened to have the right aircraft at the right time.

A solution was reached and provided that the Air Force would fly barriers a couple of hundred miles off the United States coast and the Navy would handle similar operations considerably further out over the oceans. The Air Force would operate from mainland bases and the Navy would operate from bases in Newfoundland and the Azores over the Atlantic and Alaska as well as Midway Island, Cubi Bay, and the Hawaiian Islands over the Pacific. The arrangement satisfied both services and created a double line of defense. The only problem for the Air Force was that the only AEW&C design that looked promising was already being procured by the Navy. The Navy's experience with airborne radar was seen as the answer to the threat of air attacks approaching from off-shore. The pentagon planners began looking around for the airframe and hardware necessary to implement a viable airborne early warning system. The Navy had done a great deal of development on the AEW&C concept and had already begun to procure some of the new aircraft for fleet defense purposes. Under these circumstances, the top military planners and decision makers felt that it would make sense, both militarily and politically to direct the Navy to establish the new barriers out to sea. It became apparent that Lockheed found itself with simultaneous orders for these intricate and sophisticated aircraft from both the Air Force and the Navy as both services scrambled to put these Aircraft into service by 1954. The original planning was based on 24 hour day coverage of all barrier stations. The aircraft being proposed would have sufficient fuel to remain in the air over 20 hours if needed. Thus, two aircraft, each remaining on station 12 hours, could fully staff a station. Because of training and maintenance reasons it was determined that some 40 airplanes would be required to fully staff each barrier station.

Chapter 2

Surprise Argentia

I had been through Boot Camp at Great Lakes, Illinois, went to Aviation Basic schooling at Norman Oklahoma and had just graduated from Aviation Electronics Technician "A" school in Memphis, Tennessee. Following "A" School graduation I took two weeks' leave and headed home. I was looking forward to going home for a while and spending time with my fiancé Sam and my family. While in Memphis I had received letters from my mother and my buddies saying they had seen Sam with another guy. When I talked with Sam she never said anything about it and our relationship seemed solid. After getting home I confronted her directly and sure enough she admitted that she had been seeing someone else while I was away. One thing led to another and we decided that we would go our separate ways. We broke the engagement. It was a bitter pill to swallow as I had completed the toughest part of the Navy and was looking forward to our getting married, but as it turned out it was the best thing for me in the long run.

I had just spent a great Labor Day weekend at Bob Batch's house in the Washington DC area. I graduated from high school with Bob. We had been good friends since the 9th grade. His Dad had been an engineer at WJW radio in Cleveland, Ohio. He worked with a Disk Jockey named Joe Finan at the station. Bobby and I used to review records for Finan and picked records for him to play. Since we were in high school, we represented the radio market place Finan was focused on. We reviewed hundreds of records and made our suggestions. Joe Finan played our selections. Apparently Joe Finan got caught taking bribes from the record companies to play their records. The newspapers called it payola. Bob's dad being Finan's engineer was included in the investigation and was let go when Finan was fired. Following graduation from high school Bobby's dad found a radio engineer's job at Voice of America in Washington D.C. The whole family moved to Silver Springs, Maryland. Bobby applied at the University of Maryland and started college there that September.

When I got to Memphis and started "A" school, we were told that the people with the highest grades at graduation would have an opportunity to pick either the east or west coast for their next duty station. Knowing Batch was living in Silver Springs, Maryland I picked the east coast. Following graduation when I opened my orders I was ecstatic. I was assigned to Air Early Warning Squadron 11 (VW-11) located at Naval Air Station Patuxent River, which is located at Lexington Park, Maryland. Lexington Park is located about 45 miles southeast of Washington DC. What good fortune I had. I would be spending a lot of time with Batch and his University of Maryland friends and living at one of the Navy's best duty stations. NAS Patuxent River is located on the Chesapeake Bay. Following a great Labor Day weekend of partying with Bob and his college friends around Washington and the University of Maryland campus, Batch drove me to Patuxent River to check in on Labor Day evening.

Once we arrived at the gate, I asked the Marine standing watch at the gate for directions to Air Early Warning Squadron-11. In typical Marine fashion, he replied. "You mean AEWRON-11 or VW-11 don't you?" he asked.

"I guess so," I responded.

"Well Sailor, just meander down the road from the gate for about 3 miles; at the third road turn left and you'll see the hangar on the right. That will get you there," he finished.

"Just great, these military people, they sure use acronyms for everything, AEWRON-11 or VW-11," I said sarcastically to Bob. "Down the road three miles and turn left at the third road. Magically the hangar will appear. Typical jarhead," I continued.

Off we went. We arrived at the hangar at 1700. The Marine's directions were right. I had to check in no later than 1800 hours. Once we found the hangar location, I thanked him, "Bob, thanks for a great weekend. As soon as I get settled here and figure out what my schedule is, I will call you and make plans for next week. Will that be ok?" I asked.

"No problem. I'm sure my mom and dad won't mind and my grandmother thinks you're the greatest," he replied, "I'll work on some girls for next weekend. You can stay at my house. You get to Silver Springs and I'll bring you back to the base. Have a good week. See you then."

He turned the car around waved and off he went.

I grabbed my seabag and asked the first sailor I saw close by the hangar, "Where is the AEWRON-11 Officer of the Day's (OD) office? I'm checking in."

He replied, "Yea, I knew you were new here when you said AEWRON-11. For short, we say VW-11. Just walk into that hangar door there on the left and once you get inside turn right and walk to the wall. Turn left and you will see the office about halfway down the wall. It will be marked OD office. Walk in and someone will take care of you."

"Thanks, and by the way," I asked, "What is that airplane parked over there by the side of the hangar?"

He replied, "That's a Willy Victor, the Navy name for the aircraft."

"A what?" I asked.

"That is a Super Connie. That's the plane that VW-11 flies. It's getting ready to go to Argentia, Newfoundland where VW-11 is now deployed," he said.

Not thinking as he was talking, I was looking over the plane. It was very large in my mind's eye. It was propeller driven, with four engines and three tails. The plane looked liked a pregnant banana with a big bubble under its wing, and what looked like a tower on its top. Wow! is all I could think of.

"Thanks for the help," I said. "Getting ready to leave for where?"

"Argentia, Newfoundland. No problem. I have seen a number of folks checking in today."

I opened the door and walked into the hangar and went looking for the OD's office. I found the door, knocked and went in when someone said "Enter." There sitting behind a desk was a 1st Lieutenant. He looked up and said, "May I help you?"

I saluted and replied "Yes, Sir. I am Airman Bruce Jarvis. I'm checking in for duty with AEWRON-11. Here are my orders."

He returned my salute and said, "You mean VW-11."

I replied, "Yes, Sir."

He opened my orders, read them carefully checked a list of names on his desk and said, "Well, you are in luck. VW-11 is deployed in Argentia, Newfoundland and you are headed there tonight."

"What? Tonight?" I exclaimed.

"Yes, tonight," he continued. "That aircraft sitting there outside the hangar (as he pointed over his shoulder through the window) will be leaving in about one hour or so for Argentia."

I'm sure he noticed my surprise, but made no note of it. "Here are your orders, good luck in your new assignment, and have a good trip. There is a small room just next to the office where you can wait for the plane. At about 1930 hours the flight crew will let you begin boarding the plane. They will provide you with a box lunch for dinner. The flight will be about 6 hours or so depending on the weather up north. Any questions?"

"Yes, Sir, I do have a few. In all due respect sir, I thought that I was supposed to be stationed at Patuxent River. Why am I going to Newfoundland? I don't even know where that is. How can I reach my parents and friends to let them know where I'm going?"

My mind was racing; a hole in the pit of my stomach was growing larger and larger. Other than a ride in a Piper J-Cub on my 10th Birthday, I had never been on an airplane. Now I was going to Newfoundland on a pregnant banana in less than an hour. To say the least I was a bit scared. Although, being a macho sailor, I didn't want to appear that way. It was warm in the hangar and I was sweating.

The OD was smiling, "Are you a bit nervous?" he asked. "I understand."

Patiently, he then answered my questions, "VW-11 is home based here at Patuxent River, but VW-11 is part of a rotational deployment to Argentia, Newfoundland with two other squadrons, VW-13 and VW-15. Hence, you're leaving for Argentia tonight. When VW-11 returns to the states you will be stationed here."

As to the location of Newfoundland, he pointed to an Island north of New Brunswick Canada on a map pinned to a wall behind his desk. He indicated that Newfoundland is a province of Canada. He explained that there were no phones available to call anyone at this time but, once you arrive at Argentia you will be able to contact whomever you like from there. He checked his watch and said, "Here are your orders. Check in with the OD in Argentia. Someone from his office will meet the new guys at the hanger. You best get moving as the crew is loading the plane. Take your seabag with you when you start to board and the crew will store it for you. Good luck."

"Thank you, Sir," I said. I saluted him and left the office.

All I could do at that point was to get ready to board the plane. I really felt empty, same scenario as boot camp except this time at Patuxent River. I couldn't call my Dad, or Batch. I didn't know what was in store for me the next 6 hours let alone the next two years. What will I be doing? Where am I headed? I had nothing but a lot of questions and anxiety. As I approached the plane and climbed the ladder to the hatch, I realized just how big this airplane really is.

Chapter 3

First Flight

As I entered the aircraft, I looked to the right and the passageway narrowed toward the tail. I looked left and there were 8 rows of 6 airline type seats stretching from the hatch forward toward the wing. It looked as if the plane had been modified somewhat to handle passengers. I was told to pick a seat and get comfortable as the plane would be leaving shortly. There were no windows that I could see except up front in the cockpit. The windows were too far away to see anything. During the next ten minutes the seats filled up.

"Fasten your seat belts," said a crewman. I did and introduced myself to the Chief Petty Officer in the seat to my right and asked if he had been to Argentia before.

"Yes," he said and shook my extended right hand. His name was Jack Spencer.

"I have been home on emergency leave. My mother just passed away. The Red Cross contacted my Commanding Officer who authorized the leave and I went home. I have been gone for two weeks. How about you?" he asked.

"I am sorry to hear of your loss. No, never been to Argentia. If the OD didn't show me on a map where it was, I wouldn't have any idea where the place was. I'm just reporting to VW-11," I replied. "What a surprise to me!" I continued. I then explained the situation to him.

He laughed and said "This is the way the Navy works. You never know what tomorrow brings. Not much in Argentia but trees, newfies, and fog. VW-11 deployed there about two months ago. The squadron will be in Argentia until just after the middle of December."

About that time the hatch was closed and the pilot announced he was starting engines and that we would be taking off in about 15 minutes. I heard the engines start and the noise level picked up accordingly. Box lunches were passed out and we began to taxi. Jack and I continued to talk. "What is a newfie?" I asked.

"A newfie is what we call the locals," he answered my question. "It is short for Newfoundlander."

"What is Argentia's mission? What role does VW-11 play?" continuing with my questions. He was explaining what was being done in Argentia, when the Aircraft stopped taxiing and the engine's sound increased. Noticing my anxiety Jack explained that before taking off each engines is run up to maximum power to make sure they were functioning properly.

The engine sound decreased and the pilot announced we had approval for take-off. The aircraft moved forward and turned right onto the runway. The engine's sound level increased, the pilot released the brakes and down the runway we went. I felt the runway bumps as the plane's speed increased and then I felt the plane lift off and we were airborne. The pilot then turned the plane right and headed north to Argentia, Newfoundland. My knuckles were white holding onto the seat rests. Up the plane went. We were off to Argentia. I looked at my watch. Take-off time was about 1900 hours.

Once airborne, I asked Jack what he did at Argentia. He explained, "I am a flight engineer on one of these birds. Part of VW-11 Crew number fourteen. I have been assigned to VW-11 for about three years. He was about to tell me about the airplane when I interrupted him.

"What is VW11's mission?" I asked. Here I was, assigned to an organization and had no idea what it did.

Jack was quick to answer, "The squadron's mission is to fly the barrier. The barrier is an extension of the DEW (Defense Early Warning) line."

"What's the DEW line?" I asked.

"The DEW is a line of virtual defense for North America that starts somewhere in the Pacific Ocean and continues with radar stations that run from Alaska across Canada and extends across the Atlantic Ocean. We fly the extension over the Atlantic Ocean. There are other VW squadrons that fly the barrier in the Pacific. The barrier is flown seven days per week, twenty four hours per day, three hundred and sixty five days per year. Aircraft such as the one we are on now with radar scopes replacing the seats are what we use to fly the barrier. The aircraft we are flying is called Super Connie or its official Navy designation WV or Willy Victor. This aircraft is built by Lockheed Aircraft Corporation for the Navy."

All I could say was "Wow!"

The Chief asked me what my rate was.

"ATN" I replied. "I just completed Aviation Electronics School at Memphis, Tennessee."

"You will probably be attached to the radio shop," he said.

I then asked, "Do radio shop people fly?"

"They certainly do," he commented. "There are two radio operators on each crew."

Wide eyed by now, I continued with more questions. "How large is a crew? How often do they fly? How long is a barrier flight? How do you become a crew member? I hope I'm not boring you. This is all new to me and very exciting. I'm like a kid in a candy shop. When I joined the Navy I told the recruiter I wanted to fly."

"Whoa, sailor," the Chief said. "One question at a time. We have 6 or 7 hours of flying time ahead of us. I'll try to answer some of them, but you might want to get the radio shop Chief's answers to your radio shop questions."

The Chief continued, "The Willy Victor crews in VW-11 vary from twenty two to twenty-four personnel in each crew: Three or four pilots, two navigators, two flight engineers, one electrician (the cook), two radio operators, two ACW officers, two radar technicians, and eight ACW operators.

"The electrician is the cook," I interrupted.

"Yes," the Chief explained, "He prepares the food that is eaten by the crew during each flight."

"The crew eats meals during each flight?" I commented.

He continued, "Since the duration of the flights is fourteen to sixteen hours, meals are served."

"Amazing, I never thought of that," I said.

He continued his explanation of crew size.

I interrupted, "This can change on a flight by flight basis depending on who is flying just to get their flight hours in every month."

"What does 'getting their flight hours' in mean?" I asked.

"Oh, I forgot, you're a rookie. Some personnel are paid flight pay every month, but are not assigned to a flight crew. They receive flight pay monthly like the crews do but, they need at least 4 flying hours monthly to get the pay. These personnel spend most of their month working in offices and shops and can be used as backup flight personnel when flight crew members are on leave. It also is a way for desk bound pilots to keep their wings while on an administrative assignment."

"Very interesting," I responded.

"Crews rotate their flying with other crews. We have 20 crews in VW-11. The schedule is made up by the Operations officer. The schedule works this way. Each crew gets the day off before a flight, flies one barrier, then gets a day off following the flight. This continues for three flights and following the third the crew gets three days off and the schedule begins again. After this rotation goes three times the crew then spends a week in their administrative functions. That may be in the shop for maintenance operations, office work, training, etc. Crews should be limited to about one hundred to one hundred and twenty flight hours per month. Sometimes that is exceeded. It's a target."

"Seems like a lot of time off," I commented, "What does one do in their spare time?"

"When you are on that type of flying schedule, it doesn't seem like a lot of time off. It seems like you are always in the air," Jack explained. "The reason I say that is each barrier flight time is about twelve to sixteen hours in duration. That does not include briefing and de-briefing time."

"Sounds like a challenge and adventure," I commented.

I was very excited about the barrier. I had to go to the head. I excused myself and headed toward the back of the plane. I pushed back the curtain and there it was, a port-a-potty. What did I expect on a Navy plane?

I went back to my seat and asked Jack "Where can I get something to drink to go with our box lunch?"

He motioned forward, "Go past the wing and there should be some water at the cook's station."

"A cook's station?" I asked

"Yes," Jack said. "You'll find it on the right side. There should be two jugs."

"Thanks, Chief," I replied and headed toward the front of the plane.

I walked past what looked like a complex panel on the left and then a crewman sitting in a seat located over the wing on the left next to a window. He was operating a telegraph looking key. I glanced out the window as I went past him. It was getting dark and the sun was setting. It looked beautiful to me. Across from the crewman was another complex station. There was a window there also. Both windows looked out over a wing. You could see two engines on each wing with the exhausts that were red with heat and spewing what looked like blue fire.

I continued forward and sure enough there were the water jugs on the right side of the plane just past this crewman's location. I looked forward toward the cockpit and on the left right behind me was a table with a bench seat on each side of it. Above the table was what looked like a bunk. Forward of the table were two airline type seats and across the aisle were two more. Forward of the seats were what looked like two bunks on either side of the plane. Beyond the bunks was the cockpit. I was fascinated with the aircraft and all the facilities it had.

I took a cup from the holder mounted on the wall and pushed a button on the jug. The water tasted a little stale, but after I took a drink I filled the cup again and started back to my seat. I had a lot more questions for the Chief, but when I found my seat again, he was sleeping. I sat down and ate my box lunch. It contained a roast beef sandwich, bag of chips, an apple and two chocolate chip cookies. I looked at my watch. It was about 2130. How fast two and a half hours had gone.

My head was spinning a bit. I had a lot of new information to digest and an interesting future ahead. I must have been very tired. The combination of the surprise of leaving for Argentia so quickly, the anticipation of flying on a large strange plane, and then the information about the mission exhausted me. I was whipped. As I sat down I looked around and recognized the atmosphere I was in for the last couple of hours. Inside a military aircraft with nothing in it but equipment to supplement the mission it was used to flying with the exception of the seats we were all sitting on. Little did I know what or where I was doing or going when this whole adventure began. It was almost surreal. My head was spinning and it was almost incomprehensible to me. I must have been very tired as I began dozing off. The plane bumped and I woke up quickly. But I looked around and saw that most of my fellow sailors were sleeping. I laid my head back down made sure I was strapped in, and must have fallen asleep very quickly. I began dreaming about what I went through over the last two years to get here. Who would have thought this would have happened when I graduated from high school?

Chapter 4

Reality

My dream took me back to the day that the reality of life hit me like a bomb. It happened during the middle of August, 1956, two weeks before I was to leave for Ohio University. My father advised me that he couldn't afford to send me to college. "There is no money for college. You will have to find a job or do something else," he said.

All I could say was, "What do you mean you can't afford to send me to college? I'm supposed to leave in two weeks for Ohio University. Have you told my mother? I thought that my going to college was part of the divorce agreement. Why did you wait so long to tell me?" I never got an answer to my questions.

This was a wake up call that totally devastated me. Unhappiness doesn't begin to describe how I felt. My dreams of being a football coach were shattered. I had no experience that would get me a job. I had only worked as a packer in a super market and at a car wash one summer. In 1956 you went to college, got married, or got drafted. I wasn't going to college and even though I was engaged, getting married soon was out of the question. What was left, the draft! What near future was in sight for me? The United States just ended the Korean War in the early 50's and was continuing to face the Russians and Red China in the Cold War. The draft board was still very active. The draft was a real thing to all males 18 and over. After I received the news from my father, and thought about it, I asked him," Where do I go from here?"

Dad had served in the Coast Guard Auxiliary and Police Auxiliary during World War II and was up to date on what was going on in the world. His experience told him that the only advice he could give me was "Join the service." All I could think of was that poster of Uncle Sam pointing at you and saying "I want you."

What a choice I had, I thought. He advised me to "Join the Navy. That will keep you out of foxholes and the Air Force is for wimps."

He thought this was sage advice. Thinking back on the situation, I believe my Dad developed this plan for me during the summer. Why he took so long to spring it on me, to this day I can't explain it. Dad never let on until the actual last moment. Maybe it was just the cost, maybe he kept trying to find a way, but I think it was his second wife. That's another story.

With no attractive options in mind, I had to think hard. My buddy, Don, was going to enlist in the Navy late in September. He had no thoughts of college. That was his plan. He and I talked at length about what he was going to do. My first priority was to discuss this mess with my fiancé Sam. She was certainly the important person in my life and I had to let her know of the change of plans. I wasn't sure how to let her know. We had discussed college and her visiting me on weekends until we got married. All our plans revolved around college, having a family, and my coaching career. What a dilemma I was faced with. It was a bad night and I didn't sleep well. I was going to see Sam that next morning.

I planned to take Sam out swimming at the beach at Catawba Island. We spent many good times at this beach and it seemed to be the perfect place to break the bad news. After we swam and were settled on the blanket I began my sad story, "Sam, I have something I want to discuss with you." Sam in her own way said "Yes, honey, what is it?" not expecting something as large as this to come out of my mouth.

"I don't know how to begin. My Dad told me yesterday that he couldn't send me to college and recommended that I join the Navy," I said.

Her reaction was immediate "What? Why would he do that? What about college? What about you wanting to be a coach? What about our plans? What about us?" she replied. With that she broke down and began sobbing. All I could do was hug her and try to console her as best I could.

"Dad," I continued, "indicated that he could not afford to send me to college and that I needed to do something quick as I was facing the draft sooner rather than later and that I had no training to do anything. No one would hire me."

Tears continued to fill her eyes, she began to shake, and the pain she was suffering was very evident. The hole I had in my stomach welled up to the point that I was going to burst.

"Honey," she replied, "What are we going to do?"

We collapsed into each others arms and cried. "I don't know. I don't know, honey." I said. "I'm scared. I don't know what to expect. Do you get paid?

Do they feed you? Where do you get clothes? Where to you stay? How do I reach you? When would I see you? Would I ever get to college? My head is swimming with many questions and no answers and a great deal of anxiety. I haven't slept much last night. I don't want to join the Army or the Marines. I don't want to live in tents and foxholes. I thought about the Air Force and the Navy. Right now the Navy looks like the best bet. My father says that they have all sorts of training programs. Electronics is the coming field for the future. How did he know all this? Dad and I are going to the recruiter's office tomorrow."

It was the worst day of our young lives. We cried rivers of tears, we shook with distress, we didn't want to leave the safety of each other's arms. Everything was gone. What now? When I dropped Sam off that evening, she looked very sad.

She kissed me good night and said, "Go home and make a decision to do what is best for you and us."

We had cried ourselves out. My mind was going around in circles with the prospect of making a decision the next day that would change our lives more than a young man of 17 years and his intended could imagine. I didn't sleep much that night either.

The next day dawned a warm August day. As I remember, Dad made breakfast that day and asked me how I was that morning. "How are you doing?" he asked. "Did you tell Sam about your disappointment and what you were going to do?"

I said, "I'm not doing very well at all. I'm full of apprehension. Yes, I did. It was a very sad day for both of us."

Dad smiled as if he knew what happened and said, "Life is full of disappointments son and things change every day. If this is the only disappointment you have in life, I would be surprised."

I hoped he was feeling as bad as I was. I think he was glad that I was going to join the service and distance myself from Sam. I'm sure he did not want me married at 18. In his mind I was still a kid without much knowledge of what was happening in the world. I lived in a cocoon all my life as safe as a bug in a rug. No responsibility, except taking out the garbage, cutting the lawn and making sure I got to school on time. Reality at that time during my life was who I was going out with the next weekend and how much money I had to persuade my father to give me to enjoy life. I guess I really lived in a bubble. What a dummy. I felt very depressed at that moment.

When we arrived at the recruiter's office, it seemed he was waiting for me to walk in the door. "Hello, young man. What can I do for you?" he asked. My father didn't see me watching the recruiter wink at him after the introduction. I provided him my story and asked him what the Navy had available. I thought to myself since finding out I wasn't going to college, what do I want to do with the rest of my life? I had to change my entire direction. All that I had planned was gone. I had heard from my father that electronics is the coming thing and that I should get an education in the Navy, but I also wanted to fly. I flew in a Piper J Cub on my 10th birthday for 20 minutes, a birthday present from my Dad, and I was hooked on flying

Television was exploding in the fifties, color TV was just starting to come into its own, and when it broke someone had to fix it. Dad said this was the beginning of the future growth in the field of electronics and that I should get in on the ground floor. I had no idea of what the Navy could offer but, flying was one of my few criteria. I was a very naive young boy. I didn't give myself much credit but, I knew I needed to get an education and I wanted to fly. I was walking on eggs as I discussed my future with this very enthusiastic recruiter. He advised me that to get electronics training that I had to pass a number of tests with high grades. The tests were like an IQ test. The test included Mathematics, Physics, English comprehension, and so forth.

I apparently did well as the recruiter said, "Well, son, you passed with flying colors. You can pick any field you want." I picked Electronics.

Then I asked "How about flying? I want to fly."

He responded, "I can't promise you that, but I will do everything I can to get you in airplanes. I will make sure you get aviation electronics training following boot camp with a note indicating that you want to fly."

I felt good about the aviation electronics, but the fact that he didn't know a lot about Navy flying left me a little shaky. I had a promise from someone who wanted me to join his service. But, I had no choice except to accept what he said and trust him.

I then began to fill out the paper work. When the recruiter found out I was still 17, he asked when my 18th birthday was. I told him, "September 3, 1956."

He responded quickly, "If you sign the papers today, and leave for boot camp on August 30, the Navy has what is called a "kitty cruise" for young men who are not yet eighteen. That is, you will spend only three years in active service rather than four years and will be discharged the day before your 21st birthday. Isn't that great?"

What incentive. Only three years of your life instead of four. Just sign the papers today. But, I was leaving in less than two weeks. That was quicker than I had planned. Sam and I had planned to run away secretly to Maryland to get married before I left. What now? I made the decision and my Dad and I signed the papers. My Navy career would begin in two weeks. I now had to break the news to Sam and my friends that I had planned to attend college with: Tom, Dave, Pat and Batch. They were all headed to Bowling Green University and we had big plans to party. When Tom found out that I couldn't attend Ohio University, he immediately applied at Bowling Green University and was accepted.

I was feeling both elated, having an education and adventure ahead, but very downtrodden. I had a place to begin. Life was good because of the Navy, but bad in terms of my personal plans.

That evening with as much enthusiasm as I could muster, I began telling Sam, "Sam, I joined the Navy this morning. Following boot camp at Great Lakes in Illinois, whatever that is, I will be going to aviation training and aviation electronics school. I told the recruiter that I wanted to fly. The recruiter said, he would try, but couldn't promise. I will also be in the Navy three years rather than four years." I explained the kitty cruise to her. "Isn't that exciting?"

"When do you leave?" she began with emotion in her voice

The next two weeks were a blur. I let my friends know the details and started thinking about what was ahead. I have never seen my father and Sam's father happier. My father's new wife was ecstatic. Sam and I were together most of the time. I even slept on her couch. Thank heavens for her mother. Her father seemed to be happy about the whole situation. He was a drunk. He drank about two cases of beer a week. He never offered me one until the week before I was leaving.

"All I know is that I have these papers that indicate I will be leaving on a train at 900am on August 30, 1956 and going to Great Lakes Naval Station located in Chicago Illinois for boot camp. I will be there for 10 weeks. I don't know what boot camp is or what I will be doing while there," I explained to Sam. "I asked some folks about it. They told me that I would be yelled at, learning about the Navy, march and march and march. I really wonder why all of the marching. The recruiter never told me what to bring and didn't say if I needed money, a tooth brush, or anything."

All Sam could say was, "Leaving on Labor Day weekend? It doesn't make sense to me. I don't understand why they didn't give you more information. Here you are leaving in a week and will be gone for at least ten weeks and you really don't know anything about what you are going to be doing. The Navy must not be very organized. What a bunch of jerks."

The night before I left my friends Pat, Dave, Dave, Tom, their dates, Sam and I went out together to dance and drink. It was a farewell party of sorts. We had a great time. Although we were all under drinking age, every bar we went to served us whatever drink we wanted. Twenty-one was the age for hard liquor in Ohio but, we were served at every bar we went to that night. I guess I kissed all the girls that night as well as all my buddies. We danced at the Columbia ballroom until 1: 00 am.

When we left everyone wished me well and said good night. Sam and I went back to her house and slept on the couch. Thank god her mother and father were sound sleepers. Dad and his new wife picked us up at 7am to get me to the train on time. The recruiter was there at the train terminal to meet us and all of the other new enlistees going to Great Lakes. He told us that we were going to Detroit to be sworn in and then on to Chicago. While waiting for the train I paced and Sam was emotional.

Chapter 5

Welcome to Great Lakes

At 8:15am the train pulled into the terminal. A group of guys got off the train and found the recruiter. They were on their way to Great Lakes along with me. They were from the Painesville area. We introduced ourselves. There were three of them, Wheat, Tic, and Grippe, the animal. At 8:50am I kissed Sam.

She kissed me back strongly and very emotionally "I love you, I will miss you and will write you daily," she said and began to cry.

I told her that I would be in touch as soon I get settled at Great Lakes. "I will write every day. I love you. Don't worry. I will be all right."

I hugged my Dad, said goodbye to him and to his wife, and got onto the train. What a major change in lifestyle, philosophy, and maturity! What had we gotten ourselves into? We weren't able to comprehend what was going to happen to us over the next ten weeks or, in my case three years. The Cold War was going to impact our lives forever or at least until the Berlin Wall came down.

We all boarded the train. At 9:05am the train began to move. I waved goodbye to Sam and my dad and his wife. They waved back. Sam was crying and waving. I felt as if I lost my right arm. I felt a chill go down my spine. I was on my way to a life-changing experience that would start at the Navy Recruit Training Center at Great Lakes, Illinois. We introduced ourselves again and began talking about everything a bunch of guys are interested in. Girls, football, high school, why we joined the Navy, what we wanted for jobs while in the service, where we lived, girls, Geneva on the Lake, good times and bad. We were bonding, but really didn't know it.

The train pulled into the Detroit, Michigan train station after about 6 hours of traveling from Cleveland. What a gloomy train station. When we got off the train we looked for the Detroit Navy Recruiter. He saw us get off the train with packages of orders under our arms and knew who we were. He greeted us and put us on the bus. We were told that we would be heading downtown to get sworn into the Navy and pick up some other new recruits to go with us to Great Lakes.

Following the swearing in, we all received our ID numbers and tags. Mine is 516 16 24. Dog tags. We were told, "Never forget your ID number and don't lose your dog tags, ever."

"Yes," we all replied.

Then, we all congratulated ourselves as new members of the United States Navy. The recruiter introduced the Detroit recruits to us. There was Charley Jones, a tall black fellow who was married and the father of a little boy. Chuck Weiner a rather rotund and quiet fellow. Terry Mylon, with long wavy hair who thought he was hip. There was Andrew Jones a little black fellow who acted like a banty rooster. He seemed to strut everywhere he went. He talked incessantly about himself.

What a crew we were. All full of ourselves being in this man's Navy. The recruiter took us to lunch at a cafeteria in downtown Detroit. After lunch we headed back to the train station. At 3:00 pm we boarded a new train and headed to Chicago. After sharing stories with the guys from Detroit we settled in for what was supposed to be a six hour trip. Apparently the railroad route we were traveling on was all messed up. We finally got into the Chicago train station at 1:00am Saturday morning. We were tired and hungry. We all were very apprehensive as to what was happening.

Following our arrival in Chicago a sailor from Great Lakes greeted us. "You guys are 4 hours late. Where have you been?" he asked. We told him we had no idea why were late or what had happened. He said, "I have to get you to Great Lakes quickly. Let's hike to the commuter station and catch a local train to Great Lakes."

As a group we told him that we were tired and hungry and wanted to stop for some food. He said, "We don't have time to eat and you can sleep on the train." Off we went to the next station. We got on the commuter. The train looked as if it were 50 years old. It had hard straw seats, rickety cars, and no convenience. We were sure the marks on the walls of the train were made by Indian arrows. What a ride. We arrived at the Great Lakes station at about 2:30am. We were put on a bus with other recruits and taken to the transient barracks. These were barracks that were provided for folks who would not be staying permanently in them. Our orders were taken. When we arrived at the barracks we were ushered in and told to find a bunk and go to sleep. Someone would contact us in the morning.

When we walked into the barracks we were greeted by a guy in new dungarees and no hair. I asked him, "Where are the bunks and where is the bathroom?" He pointed to the bunks and said, "The head is over there down the hall."

I said, "What is the head? I asked for the bathroom."

He replied, "Rookie, the head is Navy language for the bathroom."

"Thank you," I replied and went on down the hall. As I went looking for a bunk, I passed all of these guys with no hair in new dungarees. I started to wonder. Here it is Labor Day weekend. All of my buddies are having fun. And I'm here in the middle of the night with a bunch of hairless people and not knowing anything about where I am, what I'm supposed to do and what is going to happen to me next. I fell asleep feeling kind of isolated and asking myself, what did I do to myself and Sam? I think Sam was right when she said, "What a bunch of jerks."

I awoke to some jerk running a coke bottle around the inside of a garbage can shouting, "Reveille, reveille. Everyone get up. Get out of your bunks, chow time." I looked at my watch. It was 5:30am. I had just gone to sleep.

"Hey, buddy, why are we up so early?"

He responded, "You're in boot camp. That's what they do here boot."

"Boot," I responded "What is that?"

"That's what we call newcomers in this barracks," he said.

"If I'm a boot, what are you without hair and new dungarees?"

Proudly he said, "I'm a skinhead with ironed shirts. We have started processing and will be assigned to a company Tuesday and headed to our company barracks. You new guys are lowlife around here."

"Lowlife," I answered. "What do you mean?"

He responded, "Everyone here is rated as to how long you are here. New guys are considered lower than whale shit. That's you and your buddies who arrived here last night. You'll see the next two days before you start processing."

I asked one of the hairless guys dressed in new dungarees where the restaurant was, so we could get breakfast. He looked at me strangely and told me, "Restaurant, hell. The chow hall is down the road a piece. We don't have restaurants here, you dummy."

I asked him, "By the way. What is chow?"

"Chow is what you eat. You get fed in the chow hall. To find it follow the crowd, and don't forget the bathroom is called the head. The chow hall is only open from 0530 to 0700."

"What is 0530 to 0730 mean?" I asked him.

"That is military time. The military runs on a twenty four hour clock. One minute after midnight is 0001, one minute after twelve noon is 1201. Do you understand, boot?" He volunteered, "If you don't get there before 0700 you don't eat until noon, when it opens again for lunch. See you later. I'm going to chow for breakfast."

"I think so," I replied. I sure must have looked and felt silly.

I found Tic and Wheat and Grippe and told them what I learned. Grippe frowned when I explained military time. We were all hungry and found some skinheads to follow and found the chow hall. The line for chow was out the door and it was long. We were talking about skin heads and iron shirts and saw many of them running around standing in line with us. Grippe said, "If anyone calls me a skinhead I'm going to punch him out."

Wheat said to him, "Settle down animal. We all are going to be skinheads and iron shirts."

"I don't care what you guys say, I'll just punch them out anyhow," replied Grippe.

"You're a jerk, Grippe," chimed in Tic. "The Navy will throw you in jail and send you back to Painesville as quick as you can say whipity shit."

After fifteen minutes of waiting in line, we entered the chow hall. What a place. There must have been three or four hundred skinheads, iron shirts, and new people like us there eating breakfast. It was almost like a cafeteria. We picked up a steel tray with indentations in it for food. You had the choice of what kind of eggs you wanted; scrambled, over easy or sunny side up. Something poured over toast. I found out later that in the Navy it was called SOS or shit on a shingle. Different juices, potatoes, different types of cereals, milk, different fruits, and coffee. What a spread, I thought. My tray as well as Tic's, Wheat's and Grippe's were overflowing. We hadn't eaten for about 20 hours. Did we eat. We were full.

We left the table and took our trays to a window in the wall and left them there. There were some guys in dungarees cleaning and scraping the trays. They were taking the utensils, glasses, and cups and put them in containers, and placing the containers on a conveyer belt that ran through some kind of a dishwashing machine. They looked like they were working very hard and were very sweaty. I knew I didn't want that kind of job.

Following morning chow we all headed back to the barracks. We agreed that if the food here in boot camp is always this good, we would be very happy about that. When I got back to the barracks, all I wanted to do was to call Sam, and let her know where I was, what was happening to me, and then take a nap. I was tired. I asked the first skinhead I saw when a got back, "Where is the telephone? I need to call my girl."

All he could do was laugh. "Are you nuts, boot? You think they are going to let you make a phone call? Not only no, but hell no. All you can do is write. On top of that you are restricted to the barracks until you begin processing," he blurted out.

"What you mean I can't make a phone call? What do you mean restricted to the barracks?"

"Boot, they now own your ass. You do what you are told to do and when you can do it."

"Who do I talk to? I have to make a call." At this point I was a little panicky not being able to let Sam know what was going on. "Where do I find some paper and a pencil to do that?"

"Go see the Junior Officer of the Day (JOD) in the front office just outside the door over there," he said. I was unhappy to say the least and certainly a little lost. What a mess I'm in.

I found the JOD office. I knocked on the door and walked in. He was doing some paperwork. He felt my presence, looked up and asked, "Boot, what can I do for you?"

"My name is Bruce Jarvis from Cleveland, Ohio, I need to make a phone call and let everyone at home know what is happening to me."

"Well, boot, you get no phone calls for the next seven weeks and you are restricted to this barracks until you begin processing on Tuesday. You can write a letter anytime. We have some stamps and paper you can buy. Your letter will be mailed Tuesday morning. You can leave the barracks to go to and from the chow hall. We certainly don't want you to get sick or starve."

He was very clear and concise as if he had repeated this information a thousand times which I'm sure he had. "Thanks. Where do I buy the stamps and paper?"

"Thanks, Sir," he emphasized and pointed down the hall where there was a sign saying post office.

"Thanks, Sir," I said, and headed down the hall.

This weekend was the longest holiday weekend I had ever experienced. I wrote a letter to Sam explaining what I had been through the past two days and what was ahead for the next days. All we did that week end was talk about our situation eat at the chow hall, and sleep. We talked with the skin heads about what they had gone through getting their haircuts and clothes. They told us they were told to get in line to go to the barber shop. When they arrived at the barbershop, they sat in the chair and the barber shaved their heads. They were told the cost of the haircut would be deducted from their first pay. They looked like they were scalped. We couldn't believe it.

The Junior Officer of the Day told us we would start our processing on Tuesday morning after chow. Over that weekend we became the four musketeers; Bruce, Tic, Wheat, and Grippe. We went everywhere together. What a group: no clean clothes, no showers, nothing. We managed to get through Labor Day weekend 1956. I'm sure we smelled very sweet when we started to process Tuesday morning.

Sure enough just like clockwork, following chow Tuesday morning, our names were called by some loud mouth guy in a blue uniform with three red arrowheads upside down on his right sleeve. We found out later that he was in his undress blues and was a 1st class petty officer. We were arranged in two groups of 60. Wheat and Tic were in my group and Grippe was in the other group. Apparently Grippe was split from us because his name started with a G. We were herded by group into a building to get processed. We were told to form a line and go in the first door.

Into the barber shop we went. There were eight barber chairs with a line in front of each barber. Around each was a pile of hair at least six inches deep. Each haircut took approximately 45 seconds. For the guys with the longest hair the barbers really took satisfaction taking it off. I thought some of the guys were going to cry. What a riot and, we were going to have to pay for this haircut. We were now skinheads.

As we moved into the next room we formed three lines. Each of us was given a large box. "Take off your clothes and put them in the box in front of you. All of your clothes, dummy," said the guy in blue. He then passed out black markers and said, "Put the address you want these clothes to be shipped to on the top of the box after you close it." Here we all are butt naked with no hair on our heads addressing a box for our clothes to be shipped home in.

It was a funny sight to say the least. A lot of guys were rather embarrassed standing naked in line with everyone looking at them. If you were modest at this point, you were going to find out that you had better get over it quick or you were going to be in trouble. Thank God I played sports in school as our showers were one for all and all for one. The Navy life was going to be that way, throughout our career. Once the boxes were addressed and put on the floor in front of each one of us, out the door we went still naked and heading to the next station.

It was the medical station. Shots were being given to all recruits. We went through a gauntlet of sailors giving shots in both arms at the same time. I don't know what the shots were but we got them all. Eight pairs I remember. Guys in front of me were passing out and falling down. Apparently they never got shots before or just couldn't take it. Yes, it hurt a little, but not that bad. At least I didn't think so.

Into the next station we went. It was the clothes line. Finally, we get some clothes. We were handed a khaki bag to put our clothes in and then went to the next stop-underwear. The guy handing out the underwear looked at me and said, "Looks like medium," and threw six boxer shorts and six T-shirts at me and continued, "Put on a set of skivvies and move on."

"What are skivvies?" I thought. They must be underwear. What a name for underwear. Then it was socks six pair, dungarees three pairs, blues, two pair undress blues, one pair dress blues, three white hats, one blue hat, three sets of whites, one pea coat, one raincoat, one watch cap, 2 pair of black shoes, one pair of boondocks, one pair of spats, six hankies, one turtle neck sweater, one pair of gloves, one wool bathing suit, two neckerchiefs, three large towels, three small towels, two wash clothes, two bed sheets(called fart sacks), and two pillow cases. What a load. All of this had to fit in the bag (scabag) they gave us up front. We all looked like we had just participated in a fire sale at Macy's.

The next room was the marking room, dressing room, and packing room. We were yelled at again and told, "Go to the open window in the wall and get a stencil with your name and identity number, a black marker, and a set of stenciling instructions. Follow instructions for stenciling your clothes very carefully and don't make any mistakes stenciling. Then stencil all clothes, and when you are finished stenciling, dress in one set of skivies, dungarees, stockings, boondocks, white hat and a handkerchief. Don't lose anything because they won't be replaced for six weeks and you will have to pay for the replacements."

This all came in one breath. He continued, "Following this exercise you will go to chow. You will return here at no later than 1300 hours. Get your butts moving I want assholes and elbows."

"1300 hours, assholes and elbows, what does that mean?" I asked myself.

Well one of the recruits asked the man in blue the same question. He responded very loudly and sarcastically, "What do you mean, what does 1300 hours and assholes and elbows mean, you jerk, you're in the Navy, man. For the first and last time it means 1pm in civilian time, idiot, and get your ass moving and complete the task quickly numnuts."

The recruit meekly whispered, "Thank you."

Glad I didn't ask that question, I thought to myself. After about two hours we finished with our work. I found Tic and Wheat and we headed to chow. We were skin heads and iron shirts and were we proud. Although the clothes didn't fit right and the boondocks hurt a little, we walked proudly along. We had been processed. What comes next? After chow we were directed to a large building and told to sit down in front of the large box in front of us. After we waited about ten minutes we were introduced to our Company Commander.

Chapter 6

The Company Commander
Welcome to the Navy

He walked in by himself and stepped up on the box in front of us. He was dressed in his dress blues. His chest was packed with medals and his shoes were spit shined. He looked 10 feet tall to me. As it turned out, he was only five feet six inches tall.

He introduced himself, "My name is E. C. Landis, Quartermaster 1st class. You are assigned to Company 553. I will be with you all for the next ten weeks. When you refer to me I am Mr. Landis sir. Before you speak to me, I am to be saluted. When I return your salute, you will then speak. When our conversation is over, you will salute me and thank me by saying thank you Mr. Landis sir. I will teach you what the Navy is all about. I will teach you Navy protocols, I will teach you to march, I will teach you to respect all Navy Senior Petty Officers and Naval Officers. If you have a problem, I want to know about it. I expect that Company 553 will be the best company this Recruit Command has ever seen. If you have a problem with that statement, raise your hand." No one moved or stirred.

"Do you all understand?"

"Yes, Mr. Landis sir," we responded weakly.

"I didn't hear you," he shouted.

"Yes, Mr. Landis sir," we shouted.

Boot camp had begun holy moly, what are we in for? That is all I could think about. Following a number of expletives and movement of people Mr. Landis sir finally arranged us in company formation. He told us, "We are going to march from here on main side over to the Great Lakes Recruit Training Center. You won't see this side of the base until you graduate. For those of you who don't know your left from your right, let's all raise our right hand."

All of us but eight raised their right hand. The rest raised their left hand.

Mr. Landis sir advised the eight, "You idiots who don't know right from left step up to the front of the company."

He then took the right hand of each recruit and raised it for them. "Now, this is your right hand. Do you see it? Do you know it? Now, you jerks let's do it again. Raise your right hand."

They all did it right. I don't know what would have happened if someone would have raised their left hand. "Now," he went on, "When I say forward march, you start with your left foot and continue to march until I say halt."

He then demonstrated how to start and stop marching. "Try to stay behind the person in front of you. Try to keep the line you are in straight by looking right and left periodically. If you lose step, skip to catch up."

He then took some of the recruits and demonstrated. "Do you all understand?!!" he shouted.

"Yes, Mr. Landis sir," we yelled in return.

"Now, I'm going to show you all how to stand at attention." He demonstrated. "When I say attention, you all do it like I showed you. Attention," he shouted and we all stood at attention. "That is a start," he said. "All right, try to line up." There was a lot of shuffling and stretching out arms to line up straight. Mr. Landis sir walked through the ranks and lined people up and then stood back and looked at the formation.

"It will have to do," he noted and shouted "Attention!! Forward March!!"

Off we went a group of 60 recruits. Mr. Landis sir moving around the group, straightening, moving people, calling cadence "left, right, you recruit, get in step, look to your left, move to the right. You, jerk, look where you're going, pay attention." I'm sure he knew he had a lot of work to do.

We reached the recruit training area in about 30 minutes, still marching, looking better than when we started. We began to move down an asphalt street between buildings two stories high about 100 feet long and about 40 feet deep. There was line after line of them. They looked as if they were abandoned for a long period of time. We found out later that they had not been used since 1946. About 10 minutes later Mr. Landis sir shouted, "Halt."

We stopped. "Relax in place," he said. "Turn to the left, gentleman. Here is home for the next ten weeks. You will be billeted on the 2nd floor. This building housed recruits during World War II. I want you all to make it look like brand new before you go to sleep tonight. All the materials you need are provided on the second floor."

"Chow is at 1700 hours. Take a break for chow and be back no later than 1745. I will inspect the barracks at 2000 hours. If your quarters do not pass inspection at 2000 hours, you will work until it does. No matter what the time may be. Remember reveille is at 0530 hours. Turn to gentleman, assholes and elbows. I will be back at 2000 hours."

We all ran inside to see what our new home looked like. Was it a mess! Cobwebs on the windows and in the corners, steel double bunks and lockers piled at one end of the building, crud and dirt on the floors, the bathrooms and commode room were filthy, the showers were corroded, windows were so dirty you couldn't see out of them. What a mess.

We had about two hours to clean the place up. We broke ourselves up into groups. One group for the bathroom, one for the commode room, one group for the showers and sinks, one group for the windows, and one group for the floors and walls. We were provided with rags, brushes, and sand soap to clean the whole place. Sand soap looked and felt like LAVA soap with sand included in the bar. We had mops and a bucket of wax for the floors. We all worked on our pieces of the building. We rearranged the bunks into rows on both sides of the room. It was chow time and we all went to eat.

About 1945 hours we all got together to check out the barracks and the work we had done. The place looked pretty good to all of us. We felt good as a group about the place called home for the next ten weeks.

Right on time at 2000 hours, Mr. Landis sir came up the steps into the room. We were about to learn a lesson that we never forgot. The first time you do something in the Navy does not always meet the standards expected. Mr. Landis sir walked around the room and looked everywhere. We had left dust on top of the window frames. We left wax marks on the floor. The sinks, shower, and commodes still had a little cleaning water on them. He didn't like the way the beds were lined up with their accompanying lockers. The windows had streaks on them. The brass on the door handle was not polished. After he yelled at the top of his voice about all of these items, he opened the faucets, turned on the showers, scuffed up the floors, turned over bunks, lockers, and poured buckets of dirty water we had left in the hall, all over our clean floor. He told us in no uncertain terms "You fucking boots will learn to do it right or over and over again until it is. Now God damn it, get this place cleaned up by 2130 hours. I will be back to inspect again." Out he stomped.

We looked at each other and started to clean up the mess he made and we made sure that eight or ten of us inspected the place very thoroughly as we went through the barracks. This time we were ready for him. Sure enough back he came right at 2130 hours and did his inspection. We had picked our bunk locations and waited at them accordingly. A number of us went with him to see what would happen. I think I saw a weak smile and wink from him as he went through the barracks. When he was finished, he said, "Attention."

We snapped to attention the best we could. He continued, "This is much better. Not perfect by any means, it doesn't shine to my standards, but it will do for tonight. Now, outside in front of your barracks is a flatbed truck loaded with mattresses, pillows, and blankets. Everyone pick up one of each and return to your bunks." We all headed outside. Sure enough there was the truck. I was disappointed that the mattresses were straw stuffed as were the pillows. The blankets were wool and colored grey. We all returned to our bunks. Mr. Landis sir then demonstrated how to put your fart sack (sheet) his word, on the mattress and how the pillow case went on the pillow. He then made up a bunk and folded the blanket. He was very clear as to how it should be done. In a loud tone of voice, "The end of the pillow case is to be folded under this way, the fart sack is to be as tight as a drumhead. You should be able to bounce a quarter on the fart sack and it should bounce at least 6 inches high. The blanket is folded this way. When you get up in the morning and make up your bunk, it should look this way. Do you all understand?"

We responded very loudly, "Yes, Mr. Landis sir."

"Good. Now clean up, place your sea bags at the end of your bunks and make your bunks up. It's lights out in 10 minutes. Reveille is at 0500. Good night." And out he went.

I looked at my watch, it was 2300 hours. It was a long day for all of us. I slept like a log that night. 0530 came early the next morning with someone running the coke bottle around the inside of the garbage can. The daily morning ritual began.

Company 553 had ten weeks ahead of Recruit Training. The training was rigorous and demanding. Our training was planned to develop strength and character, loyalty, and patriotism. It was done to prepare the individual to defend America, its ideals and people, against any foreign aggressor. It certainly accomplished its mission with me and I'm sure it did for most, if not all, of my company mates.

Training was broken down into seven sections: Indoctrination, Ordinance and Gunnery, Seamanship, Damage control, Physical training, Military drill, and Ships work. Interspersed in between these efforts were Barracks life, and Religion. Your learning curve was straight up. Each area was emphasized and re-emphasized. Repeat until you get it right. This was not only an individual effort, but a team effort. Team awards were given as flags to companies for learning achievement, military drill, athletics, barracks and personnel inspection, and overall company performance.

The importance of company performance in these areas was stressed by Mr. Landis sir our second day under his leadership. "Company 553 will be the best company in all aspects of training. I will make sure you numb nuts will be the best or my name isn't Landis."

I'm sure he was being personally measured for his company's success in all these areas. He certainly meant it. We worked and marched and marched and worked.

Boot camp transitions each of the individuals from civilian life to military life. It covers the reverence for naval customs, traditions and spirit-de-corps necessary for each sailor. Further, building of personal pride in one's self is stressed in order to promote high standards of responsibility, conduct, manners and morals. These standards promote and focus the boot on the understanding of team work and the responsibility of the individual toward his shipmates and ship. Advancement is a measure of success in the Navy. These objectives work to indoctrinate the boot in his desire for self-improvement and advancement.

Mr. Landis sir made sure we understood what the Navy expected from each of us. He demonstrated to us early on how to make our racks up when we left the barracks each morning. The second day under his tutelage we found our mattresses, pillows and blankets on the floor when we returned. His comments were, "You dumb shit boots. I showed you last night how to make your rack up. Now, make them up again properly. I'll be back in 15 minutes to inspect."

He only threw ten mattresses on the barracks floor the second time. "The ten of you have five minutes to get those racks made up correctly or everyone's gear will be on the deck."

We learned a major lesson regarding Mr. Landis' method of operation. Everyone will pay if someone in the company errs in a company participation function. It was his way to instill Navy standards of self, team and shipmate. This lesson paid off very quickly for the company. We learned how to dress daily, how to function as a team, how to use the locker you were assigned, how to fold your clothes, how to hang your clothes, how to wash your clothes without a washing machine, how to hang your clothes on a clothesline without clothes pins, how to dry your clothes, and how to wear your uniforms. We learned how to salute. Mr. Landis sir demonstrated how to salute, and asked us to try. One of our company just couldn't get it right.

"You jerk, place your hand as I showed you." After three tries the recruit got it right. "Didn't your mother teach you which is the right hand and which is the left hand?"

"Yes, Mr. Landis sir, but, I'm left handed."

"Well, now you are right handed. Practice! You are all to salute everyone who is not a boot here while you are in training."

No one dared to ask how you make that determination. I decided to salute anyone that looked like he was not a boot.

In another lesson we learned how to get all the things you own into that 3ft. by 3ft. by 12 inch locker. It was an art form. Each piece of clothing had to be folded exactly right and put in its place. That included pea coats and raincoats. If it wasn't correct you found your clothes on the floor. That first week we found a lot of clothes on the floor. We found out helping your shipmate get it correct was the way to accomplish less pain. Shaving was mandatory daily even if you never shaved or didn't think you had hair on your face. Mr. Landis sir checked every day. Also checked daily was clean underwear. When he decided to check you, you put your index finger under you t-shirt collar and he looked for dirt.

If you didn't shave he would make you dry shave your face. You learned very quickly to shave daily. If the shirt was dirty, he made you take off your shirt and everyone had to shout "dirty collar, dirty collar." He knew how to get things done properly and quickly.

Following the indoctrination phase Company 553 went through basic Ordinance and Gunnery. Among the many varied operations expected of a ship at sea is to be able to protect its country by virtue of superior fire power. This division presents to the recruits a series of classes which attempt to introduce the general types of ordinance equipment used in the Navy. We were also introduced to our rifles. We carried this equipment wherever we marched as a company. We were taught that the rifle was never called a gun. If you were caught calling your rifle a gun, you had to repeat the following in front of the company: You pointed to your rifle and said, "This is my rifle," and then you pointed to your penis and said, "This is my gun," and in company 553 you repeated this 5 times in a row. No one ever failed to learn this lesson. We went to the firing range and learned to shoot. Initially, only with 22 caliber rifles, eventually with a 45 caliber pistol.

Basic seamanship training taught recruits the language of the sea and the names, places, and uses of their new trade. Among the subjects taught was marlinspike seamanship, knot tying, steering, sounding, anchoring, and mooring. Recognition of various types of ships, their characteristics, and structures are a critical piece of this training. The recruit learned the principles of ship organization and something of their role as a member of a ship's company. We were tested at every phase of basic seamanship training.

Damage control was integrated into the recruit's training. This was done to overcome one's fear of fire, gas, biological warfare, and atomic warfare. We accomplished this by participating in fire fighting, the use of gas masks, and take cover drills. We were trained how to take care of ones self and his ship in real life training drills.

On fire fighting day we were dressed very specifically. The uniform of the day was dungarees tucked into your socks, turtle neck sweaters, and watch caps. We were taught how to put out actual fires both outside of the ship and inside a compartment on fire. Then we actually manned the hoses and put out the fires. When we got back to the barracks that day we all had black faces. Rather exciting but somewhat dangerous. We all had the opportunity to experience what wearing a gas mask felt like and what actual gas felt like when we were told to remove our masks. There was a lot of coughing and tears. Not a fun experience.

The mission of the Physical Training Division was to develop strength, ability, and endurance through mass exercises and combative sports. This was accomplished through physical training (PT) for short, both in the drill hall and on the grinder, with or without your rifle. The grinder was like a large parking lot. Company 553 spent a lot of time marching and PTing on the grinder. The effort was done in company formation and in unison. This company effort was part of the work we did to win the drill flag. This was a flag the company had to win as Mr. Landis sir told us, "You boots will win the drill flag or will stay in boot camp until you do."

It became obvious to all of us in Company 553 that you had to swim or learn to swim before you left boot camp.

"Sailors must be proficient swimmers," Mr. Landis sir told us.

Graduation from boot camp required you to be able to jump into 10 feet of water from an eight foot tower and swim a 50 foot lap in the swimming pool. We had some guys almost drown before they learned to swim and could swim the lap. Special emphasis was placed on the fundamental swim strokes, abandon ship and rescue drills, and flotation drills using inflated trousers, shirts and jumpers. With practice and technique training everyone of us had the confidence in swimming and survival skills we would need while at sea. Company 553 graduated all of its recruits on time. Mr. Landis sir made sure.

Military drills were accomplished through company drill training. This included: semaphore training, marching, and PT drills as a team. Competing against other companies in military and semaphore drilling is part of the training. This was done to develop the habits of instant response to commands and the building of "Team" spirit which are used on a daily basis. Mr. Landis sir made sure Company 553 won a Drill flag. It was practice, practice, practice. He was very proud of us when we won the flag in our 6th week.

One of the most vigorous weeks of training is called "Service Week." During this week we learned and participated in ships type work. Work included: messenger service, standing watches around the clock, working in the mess halls, sculleries, and cleaning details. This week prepares you to understand what work on a ship you don't want to do. Each of us in Company 553 was looking forward to Service Week. Why? Because following Service Week completion we got to go on our first liberty. It meant we could get off of the base and visit either Chicago or Waukegan, go to a movie, have friends visit you, or just go to the craft store, have a coke at the GEE Dunk, and make phone calls. Leave the barracks on your own. Be a person again, rather than a boot. We also knew that following Service week, there would only be three more weeks of boot camp remaining until graduation. It is also the week to prepare for sea bag inspection. Following this week we had the opportunity to leave the base to go on our first liberty. We began to start feeling like sailors. It was hard to believe that we hadn't seen a girl, or talked to a girl for 6 weeks. It was difficult to believe that we hadn't talked on the phone for weeks. We really were isolated for those weeks.

What is a GEE Dunk? The Gee Dunk was like a drug store. There was a soda fountain and places to buy candy, gum, toiletries, etc. The soda fountain had girls working the counter selling cokes, milk shakes, sodas, ice cream, phosphates, etc. It was a pleasure to visit the GEE Dunk, order a coke or something, and talk with the girls who worked there. What was liberty? Liberty was a period of time off. We had a choice of days and where we wanted to go. Our choices were Saturday or Sunday, Chicago or Waukegan. We had to be back at the base by 2300 hours on either Saturday or Sunday nights.

The week before we started Service week we received our assignments. I was assigned to mess cooking and wasn't looking forward to it. That was working in the kitchen serving food or cleaning trays, etc. There were many other assignments like cleaning garbage cans, working in the office, standing Junior Officer of the Day watches, working in the scullery, cleaning barracks, etc. I got a case of bronchitis the Saturday before the week began, so I spent 3 days during service week in the base hospital recuperating. When I returned to the company Mr. Landis sir said I should stay in barracks and wash guy's whites and keep the barracks clean. I was happy not mess cooking. I had a much better deal.

I used a garbage can filled with hot water, bleach and soap to clean the white uniforms of all the company. My effort worked and all of the whites passed seabag inspection. Seabag inspection was critical to going on liberty. If the whole company didn't pass inspection, the penalty was no liberty for anyone. We did it, but not without issues. Finally Saturday morning came and we went on liberty. I took the train to Chicago with a couple of buddies. First thing I did was to call Sam. I had to reverse the charges. Boy, was it good to hear her voice. We talked about 30 minutes. We then went to a bad part of town, bought a bottle of bourbon and proceeded to get a little drunk. We were sailors. Why not? We went to a movie and visited Walgreens on State street. It was a great place to meet girls we were told. We didn't meet any. Finally we visited a tattoo shop. For $5.00 I got a tattoo on my right shoulder. Now I was really a sailor.

The day went very quickly. We caught our 2200 train and went back to Great Lakes. What a day. The next morning we all compared tattoos. I thought mine was big. Mine was the smallest. There were eagles, birds, anchors, naked girls, and many others too hard to explain. The tattoo shops did well. And the war stories were more than could be believed, but everyone had a great liberty. Our Junior Company Commander had invited his wife to come to Chicago to visit him. She came with their baby. Those of us who took the train with him met her. Very nice lady and the baby was a picture of Charlie. I was feeling very good after liberty. Talking to Sam was great. She was saving money for our future and we were looking forward to my coming home. Life was getting better.

The next three weeks were more of the same. Company 553 won the drill, athletic, education, and training flags, much to the happiness of Mr. Landis sir. His buttons were popping as he was competing against other company commanders. We all worked on our seabags, our lockers, and the barracks to make sure we all would graduate. Seabag inspection preparations were tough. Bunks were moved and everyone had to lay out their seabag on their blanket which was on the floor in front of them in a very specific format. All of the clothes were laid on the blanket. Mr. Landis sir went through each seabag with a fine toothed comb. If there was a mistake, clothes not folded correctly, clothes not clean, or clothes missing, he picked up the blanket on the end and tossed it up in the air. What a mess and an embarrassing situation for the one whose bag was wrong. Do it again. Wash those clothes. Fold them right. Place the stuff in the right spot.

The whole company had to be perfect for the final evaluation and graduation. It took a great bit of practice, but when final inspection took place Company 553 was perfect. Mr. Landis Sir was proud of us. The last week was difficult as everyone was looking forward to Friday morning. We were inspected, the barracks was inspected, and the sea bags were inspected and checked twice.

Payday had been accomplished and there was a lot of money in the barracks. No one other than Company 553 personnel was allowed in the barracks. Tickets were processed and handed out. Orders were completed and provided to each graduate. We all found out where we were going and what our rates would be. The aviation sailors (those going to the aviation side of the Navy) received their dress and undress blues with three green stripes. We were Airman. The

Black shoe Navy sailors (those going to the ship board side of the Navy) received their dress blues and undress blues with three white stripes. They were seaman. How proud we were.

Graduation ceremonies were spectacular. During the summer graduating companies marched to the main side of Great Lakes Navy Station and graduated on the main parade ground Ross Field. But since it was winter Company 553 graduated in the large drill hall. Graduation was special as families and friends were able to attend. We marched without our Company Commanders with march music played by the recruit band and bugle core with all the flags flying and pomp and circumstance in great order. Everything was perfect. The Admiral gave his graduation speech and wished us all fair winds and following seas. Marching in the revue gave me goose bumps and I'm sure my fellow company members felt the same way. We had accomplished the first phase of our Navy careers. We were sailors now. We were on the way to the fleet.

After the formal ceremonies we marched back to the barracks to pick up our gear, say good bye to our buddies and Mr. Landis sir. Mr. Landis told us we no longer had to salute him or any other enlisted personnel. He told us how proud we made him of us and when he said goodbye to us I thought I saw a small gleam in his eye. He taught us a lot. It was time to head to the bus, train, or airport to leave for the next base or home for leave. I picked the train to travel home to Cleveland.

Following the graduation from boot camp each recruit either is shipped to the fleet or goes on to their initial training for their rate. Rate in Navy talk is what your function in the Navy will be. What is your job or rate? Mine was Aviation Electronics Technician (AT).

Following leave those of us that were going on to the aviation side of the Navy, we all went on to basic Aviation training in Norman, Oklahoma. We were Airdales. An Airdale was the name for all sailors that were going to be assigned to the Naval Aviation. Those sailors who were non Airdales and were assigned to the fleet side of the Navy were called the Blackshoe Navy. All Airdales were assigned to Naval Station Norman Oklahoma following boot camp. Our next set of orders would come after finishing training at Norman. I knew at that point that following five weeks at Norman I would be going to Memphis, Tennessee for six months of Electronics training. All of the Blackshoes went to a ship, naval base, job training, or became a member of a ship's company. Before we went forward to training were all able to go on leave (vacation) for a week before catching a train, plane, or bus to get to the next duty station.

Chapter 7

Hello Newfoundland

I awoke with a start, the plane was bucking like a horse, and seemed to be sliding from side to side.

I was sweating bullets as I looked over at the Chief and asked him, "What is wrong? What is going on with the plane? Why is the plane moving around so violently?"

"Don't panic, sailor," he said. "We have run into a little weather over New Brunswick. The plane is very capable of managing all types of weather."

"Do you need a barf bag?" he asked.

"I don't think so," I replied.

I was thinking, what am I doing here? I had never been in a plane like this, never had such a ride except on a roller coaster. I was holding on for dear life. The smell of barf permeated the plane. Apparently a couple of other sailors had weak stomachs and puked on themselves and the plane. I guess they couldn't find a barf bag. A couple of crewmen came back to help these guys out and clean up the mess, but the smell persisted. After what seemed like hours of being tossed around, the plane leveled out again. I checked my watch and it was 0100 hours.

"When do we get there, Chief?" I asked.

"We should be there very soon. We just flew over New Brunswick," he said.

"I hope so. I'm tired of being cooped up in this cramped space with the smell of puke," I replied. I sat back and waited. In about five minutes the pilot advised us to prepare for landing. Following that announcement he came back on the speaker and advised us that we will be using a GCA to land as Argentia is fogged in.

"GCA, what is that?" I asked the Chief.

"GCA means Ground Controlled Approach. Our approach to the landing field will be under control of Ground Controllers at Argentia. Let me assure you that they are very good at their job. Argentia is fogged in about 265 days per year. They get a lot of practice."

"That's very reassuring, Chief," I responded nervously.

The pilot apparently left the inter-com speakers on as the next thing we heard was, "Eight knothole, this is Argentia ground control approach. Turn left to 270 degrees and reduce your altitude to 2000 feet."

"Roger, 8 knothole," the pilot responded.

"Keep your heading 270 degrees and remain at 2000 feet."

"Roger, 8 knothole," the pilot again responded.

"Turn left to heading 260 degrees and continue at 2000 feet. You are on glide path. There is no need for you to respond until you land. Reduce your speed and begin your descent at 200 feet per minute. You're on glide path. Turn right to 270 degrees and continue your descent, you are on glide path. Wind is North at 15 knots, ceiling is 300 feet with mist and visibility one quarter mile. You're on glide path."

About this time my knuckles were white and that hole in the pit of my stomach was opening again. We heard the engines slow and a noise I didn't comprehend. "Chief," I whispered, "What was that?"

"That is the flaps being lowered for landing," He noted.

"You're on glide path, turn left to heading 265 degrees and increase your descent to 300 feet per minute. At this point another noise, "what is that" I whispered again,

"The wheels are being lowered" he responded.

"You're on glide path. You are approaching the field, you're on glide path. You are at 300 feet and should be able to see the field."

"Roger, 8 knothole," the pilot responded. And then the wheels touched down I found out that the next noise was the pilot reversing the engines to slow our speed, and we had landed at Argentia. I was soaking wet from sweat.

I took a deep breath and said to the Chief, "We made it. It was a safe and smooth landing."

The Chief replied, "Any landing that you can walk away from is a safe landing. Welcome to Argentia."

I thanked him for answering all my questions and being so patient with me.

He said, "I was new once too. I understand the way you feel and your anxiety. Good luck in your new assignment. I'll see you around."

I looked around the plane and saw the other sailors breathe a sigh of relief. That GCA landing was scary to say the least. The plane taxied for about five minutes, turned, and the engines stopped. The hatch was opened and the person from the OD's office stepped into the plane and said "All new people checking into their duty station wait at the bottom of the ladder and I will give you directions."

I looked at my watch and it was 0320 hours. It was the middle of the night. With that we were told to leave the plane. As I left the plane it was very bright. We were inside a hangar with another plane on our left with a group of sailors working on it. Down the ladder I went and waited for the person from the OD's office. Someone called my name "Jarvis." I turned and raised my hand, said "yo" and my seabag was handed to me. As I waited about 20 other new sailors waited with me.

The Officer of the Day's staff person then started to speak, "Welcome to Argentia," he began. "My name is Carter. I will collect your orders. Move out to the front of the hangar and transportation will be waiting for you. It will take you to transient quarters. You are to check in at your duty location at 0800 this morning. The chow hall is located next to the barracks. You should be able to find your way. You will be woken up at 0630. Breakfast starts at 0530. You shouldn't be late. You can pick up transportation in the morning at the same place you will be left off tonight." He began to read off names and duty locations for each person waiting. He called, "Jarvis, radio shop."

I raised my hand and asked, "What time is it here?"

Carter responded, "0300 hours." It was one hour earlier than Eastern time. "Best get moving to the barracks," he continued, "If you want a little sleep."

We all headed toward the front of the hangar talking about what we just went through, introducing ourselves as we walked. The door was open and we walked out. It was pitch black outdoors, drizzling, and foggy. Welcome to Argentia I thought. What next? There was our transportation; it was a semi-truck with a door cut into the trailer's side. The driver was waiting for us and told us to get on board. We all found seats along the wall of the trailer and the truck lurched forward. We couldn't see much except through the open door. It was a dreary night. Finally the truck stopped. The driver came around and told us, "The temporary barracks is directly up the hill with a door in the front."

We all piled out with our seabag and dragged them and ourselves up the muddy slope. We opened the door and what did we find? Well the bunks were lined up barracks style, with mattresses piled on each bunk. No sheets, but included were straw filled pillows. We all picked a bunk, placed our seabag next to our bunk and tried to get some sleep. It was going to be a very short night as 0630 hours was very near. I just laid down and shut my eyes. I didn't sleep that night, but I remembered the first night at boot camp. This was bad but that was worse. What a day. What a surprise!!!!!

Chapter 8

The Real Navy

After our arrival at Argentia, I began to learn how to work in the radio shop. After about three weeks of learning the ropes of the radio shop and how the base operated, the shop Chief told me to go upstairs in the hangar and start to learn Morse code as he was going to assign me to a crew as third radioman. He said I had to be able to copy at least 20 words per minute before I could start to fly and operate in that capacity. It took me about three weeks to become what I thought was proficient at Morse code. What a rude awakening I had when I flew as third radioman on my assigned crew the first time. The chief introduced me to the first and second radiomen of my crew. The first radioman was a first class petty officer named Jim Harris. The second was a third class petty officer named Dave Renard. Both were Aviation Electronics Technicians like me. But, I was an Airman.

My first flight with these guys was an experience. We had the 2000 hours flight on a Thursday evening. I arrived at the hangar at 1900 hours to meet Dave. He was going to teach me what a preflight was for the radio crew. He told me that Jim was at the preflight brief upstairs in the briefing room. We began our preflight in the cockpit. The first step was to check the clock time with WWV atomic clock and advised the crew that was on board at that time accordingly. We contacted Argentia tower for a Low Frequency (LF) and Ultra High Frequency (UHF) radio check and then tested the operation of Automatic Direction Finder (ADF) equipment with the local radio station. Finally we tested the intercom system and the loudspeakers throughout the aircraft.

We then moved to the radioman's station. The LF transmitter was checked for loading and its output checked by placing a lead pencil on the transmitter pole and keying the transmitter. He said if you draw an arc you are loaded properly. We definitely drew an arc of about an inch.

He cautioned, "Don't touch the transmitter pole while keying the transmitter or it will burn a hole in you and knock you across the airplane."

I understood after I saw the blue white arc from the equipment burn the end of the pencil. Dave then sent a signal to NWP7 via Morse code. NWP7 responded in code. NWP7 was the local Argentia, Newfound low frequency Morse code station that we radiomen would be communicating with during our barrier flights, local training flights, and other flights we would be participating in. He put the low frequency radio on the speaker so that I could hear the code and the response from NWP7. I was fascinated by the process and found out that there was a lot more to the process than just sending Morse code signals.

I sat with both Jim and Dave that flight and came home very tired, but comfortable with the fact that I could eventually do the radioman's job. I flew with this crew for the next three months. My Morse code improved and I sat at the key and worked my shift. I finally felt comfortable communicating with NWP7.

I soon found out that I would rather fly than work in the shop. Shop duty included working on equipment that had failed to operate and removing equipment from the airplanes we flew checking them out and replacing the equipment again. That was physical labor. The majority of radio equipment in the planes was ARC-27 UHF transceivers. They weighed about 50 lbs each and had to be carried down a 12 foot ladder to get to the ground. To remove them from the airplane one had to crawl under the main isle of the airplane in a space about 2 1/2 feet of overhead space. The ARC-27s were spread throughout the length of the airplane. There were 7 or 8 of these heavy transceivers carried by the Willy Victor. In addition to the UHF equipment there were LF receivers and transmitters, ADF equipment, intercom equipment and various other navigation aids such as Loran equipment. It was always a physical day when an aircraft was in for a 100 hour checkout.

In addition to our shop, the Radar shop had a load of equipment to check out. They were responsible for the operation of the APS 20 search radar, the APS 45 height finding radar, and the IFF equipment. The mechanic shop was responsible for engines and other physical equipment of the aircraft and they were always up to their ears in work, grease, oil, and hydraulic fluid. When the mechanics came home from work they were covered with grease. The electric shop was responsible for the automatic pilot equipment as well as the instrumentation of the aircraft and its wiring. All 100, 200, and 300 hour checkups were done by the squadron personnel. It was a large responsibility for the squadron when a plane was ready for one of these. With the hours we flew every month there was always a plane or two ready for their 100, 200, or 300 hour checkup. When an aircraft reached 400 hours of flying they were flown to Lockheed Air Service (LASI) at Idlewild airport in New York city for a complete tear down.

I was going to be in Argentia for four months. It was a learning experience. I found out that there wasn't much to do except work, fly and go to the Enlisted Men's club. This club was for those of us who were less than 21 years old. All we could drink was beer. It was ten cents a can for regular beer and fifteen cents for ale. Not much of a choice, but we found it was better than soda. They also served steak dinners for $2.50. On paydays the waitresses at the club served a lot of steak dinners. The club was the favorite place to relax and drink beer.

I met new friends, David Oyster and Gordon Knobby Knowles. What a pair these two guys were. David was from Painesville, Ohio. He joined the Navy the day he turned seventeen. He graduated from high school at sixteen. He is the only seventeen year old alcoholic I ever met. Knobby was a good ole boy from Andalusia, Alabama. We worked hard and drank hard.

One night at the club we had a drinking contest. I drank 12 beers and couldn't stand up and David drank 30 beers and took me back to the barracks. The next morning I woke up with a pounding headache. I took two aspirins and headed to the chow hall to get some coffee. I really felt bad. I went down the hill and caught the shuttle to the hangar. When I arrived at work at 0700, the shop Chief looked at me and said, "What happened to you? You look as if you died and then woke up. I have never seen someone look as bad as you do."

Are you sure you don't want to go back to the barracks and go to sleep? No you can't do that, we have two 100 hour checks to complete today. I need you to unload the ARC 27s from each aircraft, bench check them, and reinstall them in the planes. When you finish that task you can go back to the barracks."

All I could say was, "Yes Chief." That was one of the longest and trying days I ever spent in the shop. When I went back to the barracks there was David Oyster laughing and playing cards. He forgot to tell me he had the day off. I decided that I wouldn't be drinking beer with him again. I just climbed into my rack and went to sleep.

Knobby on the other hand was a good ole southern boy. He joined the Navy rather than go to jail for helping his grandfather make and deliver moonshine. Andalusia, Alabama is a small town hidden in a valley in the middle of the state. There wasn't much to do there for an eighteen year old boy. There were no jobs available so he helped the family make moonshine. Apparently the local judge felt sorry for Knobby as he gave him the choice. He made the right choice. He joined the Navy and became a radar technician.

One night after coming back to Argentia from leave, he woke me up at about 0400 to show me what he brought back with him. "Bruce, wake up and look what I brought back with me. This is pure unadulterated Knowles' white lightening. My grandfather gave it to me to share with you all. Here take a look. Look at the grubs floating around in it."

I tried to clear my senses to look at the Mason jar full of a clear liquid with tiny little specks floating in it. "Here, take a swig of it. It is smooth as silk. This is the real thing," he said. He opened the jar and handed it to me. I took the jar, lifted it to my lips and took a swig. Once I swallowed, I felt the liquid burning all the way down to my stomach. I gagged.

All Knobby could say was, "Isn't that good. Take another drink."

"Thanks, but no thanks, Knobby. I have had all I can take at this time. I'll have more at later time." He left me to go back to bed and went down the barracks to his next buddy.

It was December 15, 1957 and the squadron was preparing to go back to Patuxent River. VW-11 had finished its tour of duty in Argentia, Newfoundland for the year. It would be back to the states for a rest, training and the holidays. I was looking forward to getting back home and taking some leave. The rest of the crew were looking forward to going home, seeing their families and sleeping in their own beds. It had been an interesting four months for me. I learned what the Navy was all about. I became a radioman and began to fly regularly with a group of Navy airdales. I learned what living with a group of Navy regulars was. In addition to David and Knobby, I met a lot of new folks. I spent time with my buddy from Norman, Oklahoma Floyd Ivey, Bob Biss a buddy from Memphis, Tennessee and Tom Schofield. Bob was from the Cleveland area like I was. Tom was from Chicago and was one of Bob's friends.

Chapter 9

Return to Patuxent River

Naval Air station Patuxent River (Pax River) is located in St. Mary's County, Maryland on the Chesapeake Bay near the mouth of the Patuxent River. It was commissioned on April 1, 1943 on land mostly acquired by eminent domain. The base is located on over 6000 acres on what was prime farm land. It is situated on several large plantations in Mattapony, Susquehanna, and Cedar Point, as well as many tenant and share cropper farms and a number of vacation properties. In 1937 The Navy's Bureau of Aeronautics wanted to consolidate aviation test programs that were located on a number of other Naval Air Stations. The Cedar Point location was picked due to its remote location on the coastline with ample space for weapons testing. The onset of World War II spurred the establishment of the new air station. Rear Admiral John Henry Towers requested approval and authorization to begin construction on December 22, 1941. He received approval from Frank Knox, Secretary of the Navy, on January 7, 1942. Residents had about a month until March 1, 1942 to relocate. The Government purchased the land at a cost of $712,287.00.

Lack of transportation in St. Mary's county led the Navy to restart a Pennsylvania Railroad branch line from Brandywine to Mechanicsville, Maryland and build an extension to the base in 1944. It was used only by the US government until 1954 when it stopped operation. The highway that was being built to the new airbase was completed. At the peak of construction approximately 7000 personnel worked on the project. Workers from all over the country participated. During construction housing needs out stripped the supply and barracks were built on station for the workers. Later several housing areas were erected off station for workers and their families in the town named Jarboesville. It's name was changed to Lexington Park in honor of the USS Lexington, the Navy's second aircraft carrier lost in the Battle of the Coral Sea on May 8, 1942. It grew rapidly in response to World War II. The base became a center for testing and included the Naval Test Pilot training center in 1958 and Weapons Test Division in 1960. In 1957, Pax River was the home port for all three Airborne Early Warning Squadrons: VW-11, VW-13, and VW-15.

When we found out that we were ready to head to Patuxent River following my 4 months in Argentia, the flight engineer told all of us in the crew to buy their limit of whiskey, scotch, champagne, gin, vodka, etc. Each of us was able to legally bring a gallon of alcoholic beverage back to the states. We were leaving to go back on the 15th of December. A number of other crews had left before we did as we had to fly our last scheduled barrier on the December 13th. Going back to Patuxent River was an exciting time for everyone. We would be back for the holidays. I bought a bottle of Shalimar for Mrs. Batch and champagne for Mr. Batch, Bobby, and me. Bob's mom and dad treated me like their own on the Labor Day weekend I had stayed with them before I left for Newfoundland.

As we arrived at the hangar to board our airplane I couldn't believe what I was seeing. It looked as if the crew unloaded a whiskey store and was going to put it into the airplane going to Patuxent River. It was fascinating to watch the stuff loaded into the airplane. The radome below the fuselage was opened and 10 cases of Haig and Haig pinch scotch was loaded. The life raft compartments were opened, the rafts removed and loaded with various bottles of booze into the top. Inside the aircraft panels were removed and filled with booze. These guys were pros and had done this many times before. I'm sure the liquor cabinets of everyone and their friends were full when the plane was unloaded and the booze taken home. I bought some champagne and a couple of bottles of Canadian Club to take back. We all filled out a chit that said we were bringing back a gallon of booze to the states. The chits were for the customs agent when we arrived back at Patuxent River. The day our crew left was a beautiful sunny cool day. I could feel the anticipation the crew had as the plane left the ground. The flight was routine. As the third radioman of this crew I didn't have much to do except sit back and wait to land. I found out from Jim that flying to the States was different for the radioman. He sent out status reports to NWP7 each hour and finally signed off when we landed.

It took about 7 hours to fly to Patuxent River. When we landed the flight engineer announced on the intercom, "Gentleman, we are home. It is time to get ready for the customs man. Get out your chits and make sure they are signed. Remember only one gallon per person." When we approached the taxiway to the hangar the plane stopped. The cockpit door was opened and in came the customs man. He welcomed us home on the loud speaker system. He advised us to have our chits with the liquor we were declaring. He then walked through the airplane checking everyone to make sure they only had what they declared. He walked back to the cockpit and left the airplane with what looked like a bottle of Canadian Club whiskey.

The engines were revved and the plane headed down the ramp to the hangar. The plane stopped and pulled into the hangar. We all gathered our sea bags and the stuff we brought home and deplaned. The hangar was buzzing with people. There were wives and children welcoming their husbands and dads home following a four-six month absence, lots of hugging and kissing, sailors opening the radome and taking out the scotch. The life raft storage areas opened and the booze was removed. As we moved out of the airplane the panels inside were being removed and the whiskey was gathered and taken off of the plane. Sailors were gathering their booze and leaving the hangar. Everyone was carrying booze, seabags, luggage, carry on bags, kids, and being led by wives and girlfriends out the hangar doors.

All of a sudden it seemed that the only personnel left in the hangar were us single guys going to the barracks. What a day. I was back where I began that Labor Day weekend in September. Almost 4 months later, I was now a fleet sailor with experience. I knew how to drink and looked forward to contacting Bobby Batch and calling my dad and family. There was a bus outside of the hangar waiting for us. It took us to the barracks up the hill. As I went in I saw Bob, Tom, and Floyd. They were a welcome sight. It felt good to see them and know that I wasn't going to be alone without knowing anyone again. We knew we were going to be in Patuxent River for at least another 6 months before going back to Argentia. Let the adventure begin. It was chow time and we headed to the chow hall, wherever it was. Bob and Tom lead the way.

We were just in time for evening chow. It was great. We ate fried chicken, mashed potatoes, carrots, peas, corn, bread, and salad with apple pie for dessert. The chow in Newfoundland was good, but this was stateside chow and it was great. Food seemed better here in the states than it did in Argentia. All mental I guess. Following chow we all went back to the barracks to get settled in and unpack our bags. Christmas was coming and we were all looking forward to some rest and relaxation. I wanted to see what Patuxent River was all about and what was outside the gate. I didn't have much leave accumulated and wasn't going home for the holidays. Bob and Tommy were heading home and Floyd was missing Jo badly. We had talked about him going home. I told him "Floyd if you miss Jo so badly, go home and marry her."

"Do you think she will marry me?" he said.

"Are you kidding? If she is everything you say she is and she feels about you as you feel about her, I don't think there will be an issue. How about her parents? Will they approve?" I asked.

"I haven't asked her dad, but I don't see that as an issue. They are getting older and I think they will approve as Jo is the only one left to leave the nest," Floyd assured me. "Tomorrow I have to look for a place to live, find a car, and file my leave papers. Then I'll go home and get married." He was raring to go. He would get home for the holidays and get married soon thereafter.

Bob, Tommy, and I would be going to work tomorrow to find out what our schedule was going to be here at Patuxent River. They were heading home on leave for the holidays and I would be staying here at Patuxent River as most of the married guys were taking leave. I would be part of the skeleton group carrying on for the holidays. I didn't have a girl any longer as Sam and I had broken our engagement that past summer, so I really had no reason to head home. I called my dad. He was fine and would be spending the holidays with his wife's family. My mother was still in California with my sister Nancy Lee. As far as my dad knew they were fine. "No news is good news," he said. I told him I wouldn't be coming home for the holidays. He understood and told me to call him on Christmas. Then I called my buddy Bobby in Washington. We had a lot to talk about and we would get together on the weekend. I was really looking forward to that as Bob said we would be going to a party at the college this Saturday night. Oh, what a start. Six months of partying at the University of Maryland.

Chapter 10

Patuxent River
December 1957

We all headed to the hangar the next day. Our hangar at Patuxent River was much smaller than the hangars at Argentia, Newfoundland. Only one plane would fit in the Patuxent River hangar. This was because the planes had to be in the hangars at Argentia to be worked on and the weather in the winter was much more severe at Argentia than at Patuxent River. The radio shop was much smaller. Our Chief advised us that the schedule for working and flying would be posted in the shop as would be the squadron watch schedule.

"Chief, I will stand a watch on Christmas Eve. I won't be going on leave for Christmas or New Years." I said.

"Thanks, Jarvis. I will make sure you will be scheduled," the Chief replied.

Bob asked the Chief, "What type of flying will we be doing?"

He responded, "We will be flying four hour hops. Basically it will be for pilot training. Does anyone want to fly a lot of hops?" he continued.

About six of us raised our hands. Bob Biss, Larry Rudder, and I were included in the six. Larry was a farm boy from Missouri that we had just met. He was a definite down home type. He was going on Christmas leave to see his fiancee and plan for his wedding in June. He showed us a picture of his girl. She was a cute well built strawberry blond. You could tell she was a country girl from the dress she was wearing. Larry was very proud of her. Larry, like Bob and I, didn't like shop work either. He would rather fly.

"Ok," the chief said, "I will schedule you all as much as I can. If you have any changes about that let me know quickly as I will have to change the schedule. Most of us only want to fly our 4 hours per month when we are at home." The reason for this was that only four hours monthly were required to maintain one's flight status and receive flight pay.

We settled into a regular schedule, work in the shop and fly. December was a rather slow month as people were leaving to go on leave and the flight schedule was rather slim. In the few days prior to Christmas I flew three hops and worked in the shop the remainder. I was scheduled for a squadron watch on Christmas Eve.

The hops we flew were very different from the barriers we flew out of Argentia. The radioman's role was to provide status reports every hour. The squadron was training pilots. Most flights started with touch and goes. That is touching down as if landing the aircraft and then turning up power and taking off again. We would fly to Andrews Air Force Base, Anacostia Naval Air Station or Bolling Air Force Base to do touch and goes. This would be a great opportunity for the radioman to go up to the cockpit, stand behind the flight engineer and watch the pilot do his thing. It also gave us the opportunity to see the Washington DC area from a different perspective. From the air it is spectacular. Some days we would do 8 or 10 touch and goes at a given base or do them at multiple bases. Then we would return to Patuxent River for a few more touch and goes, land, and head to the hanger. The excitement came when aircraft stalls were being performed.

The radioman's seat looked over the port wing. There was a removable porthole next to the seat. Just up the aisle from the radioman was the navigator's position on the starboard side of the aircraft. Just down from the navigator's position across from the radioman's seat was another removable porthole. The radioman had a clear look out both portholes. Located at the navigators position was a pressure altimeter.

The radioman had a clear view of the altimeter. When the training pilot was ready to begin stall practice, we would fly out over the Chesapeake Bay and gain altitude to approximately 5000 feet. The principal pilot would tell every one on board that stall training was to begin. To stall an aircraft the pilot pulls back on the stick that controls the airplane and causes the aircraft to climb sharply. The aircraft climbs up to the point where it cannot go any higher. At that point the aircraft begins to shake violently and will fall sharply down on the starboard wing tip. At the command pilot's direction the pilot in training puts the aircraft into a stall attitude until the WV would begin to shake. I mean everything in the aircraft would begin to shake.

The WV would strain to continue to climb until it couldn't go further. The WV would turn its right wing tip 90 degrees down and the WV would begin to fall sideways straight down toward the bay. The altimeter would spin and indicate a rapid drop in altitude for 500 to a 1000 feet until the pilot pulled up the aircraft to the port and the WV would right itself and begin to regain its altitude. Your stomach would feel as if you went down a steep roller coaster hill and came back up. Once altitude was recovered slightly, up we went again to start another stall and back down again. After three stalls, I'm sure the pilots discussed the process and off we would go again.

This was one of the thrills of flying in the WV. It was great fun and the pilot trainees had the opportunity to learn how the WV would handle a stall and what was required to correct the stall. Not all of the radiomen in VW-11 shared my or Bob's enthusiasm for stalling. Following stall training we would head back to Patuxent River to do touch and goes and call it a day.

We just loved to fly. It was not only a great experience, but they paid us to do it. If we could have done it every day we would have. Following a day at the shop or a hop we would head up the hill to our barracks. Many of us would head to the TV room and watch Dick Clark and American Bandstand. This would give us time to relax, see what the latest dances were and take a nap before chow. Normally night was a time to write letters or head to the enlisted men's club to drink a few beers and play shuffle board for beers. As Christmas was getting very close most of the guys were headed home. I was preparing for a Christmas Eve watch from 2000 hours until 2400 hours.

It was Christmas Eve and I headed to the Officer of the Day office. I checked in and was read my orders and left to start my watch. I relieved the man on watch and was advised of status and given my rifle to carry with me for the next four hours. The night was clear and cool. The uniform of the day was undress blues with sweater, Pea Coat, gloves, and Watch Hat. It was very quiet that night. The watch consisted of walking smartly around two WV aircraft parked outside of the hangar and checking the outside of the hangar for anyone trying to gain access or do damage. Then I would do it again. It took about 15 minutes to complete the walk. One might think it was a boring night. Surprisingly it wasn't. My imagination exploded. First, I wondered, what would I do if the bad guys tried something. I had a rifle, but no ammunition.

I knew I had to say, "Halt who goes there?"

Then what? Run like hell? Fight with them, hollering as loud as I could? Who knows? I just thought about it, developing a strategy as to what to do. I had no idea. Be brave. Any noise I heard scared me. Fortunately, there wasn't much noise. It was Christmas Eve and only Santa Claus would be out tonight. I began to think about all of the Christmas's I celebrated as a child. I remembered they were great. Christmas was my mother's favorite time of the year. The house would be decorated beautifully. My sister and I would be very excited about Santa Claus coming to our house. My memories were vivid.

Mom would take my sister Nancy Lee and me downtown on the streetcar in Cleveland, Ohio to visit Santa Claus. This would give us the opportunity to let Santa know what we wanted for Christmas. We always looked forward to this occasion. Mom would dress us up warmly as we had to walk a couple of blocks to the streetcar stop. The streetcar would come up to us and the door would open and Nancy Lee and I would jump up the steps to get into the car and mom would put in the 15 cents it would cost us to ride downtown. We would ride by the local stores and the steel mills, and cross a couple of what looked to us to be big bridges. Our eyes were wide open and excited. Just the thought of seeing Santa Claus! Wow, what a day it is going to be. Sure enough we arrived downtown and mom would take us to Higbee's department store to see Santa. She took off our coats as soon as we entered the store so we wouldn't catch cold when we returned outside. We took the escalator. Imagine a moving stairway made out of wood. It took us to the 3rd floor where Santa hung out. When we reached his location there was a lot of noise and a lot of kids like us.

I asked Nancy Lee what she was going to ask for. "I want a yellow haired doll, an ironing board, some crayons, and a sled. What do you what?"

"Well, let's see. I want a BB gun, a bow and arrow set, baseball glove and some model airplanes," I told her.

It was now our turn to see the man. Up the ramp we went. Nancy went first. Mom made sure she sat on Santa's lap and had her picture taken. It was my turn and I did the same thing. Mom was always very attentive while were telling Santa what we wanted for Christmas. We were sure happy kids. Mom would then take us to a play area the store had for kids while their moms went somewhere. We played for what seemed like hours until mom came back for us. She would take us to lunch in the department store and we would head home. We had a lot to tell dad when he came home.

We believed in Santa coming down the chimney until both of us found out that Santa was really mom and dad. Then we helped decorate the Christmas tree. What great times we had.

I was deep in thought and almost banged my head on an antenna sticking out of the bottom of the fuselage. What wonderful thoughts of family I was having. I woke up quickly as a Jeep with bright lights rounded the corner of the hangar. The person driving the Jeep approached. When he was within shouting distance I gave the "Halt who goes there?" command and the Officer of the Day (OD) identified himself. He asked "How is it all going? Are there any problems?" I replied, "Quiet, sir." "Carry on, Merry Christmas," he replied and walked back to the Jeep to leave. What a relief.

I started to think about all the kids waiting for Santa Claus this Christmas Eve and looked up and thought I saw him on his way that clear and cool evening while I was protecting this hanger and the two Super Constellations that I was walking around. It was my first Christmas away from home and to be all alone at Patuxent River Naval Air Station was an interesting and lonely experience. Merry Christmas!!!! At 2355 the Jeep came back bringing my relief. I passed along the nightly orders. I was happy to get into the Jeep as the OD's driver took me to the barracks. I slept well that night dreaming about Christmases past.

I walked to the base chapel for Mass on Christmas morning. There weren't very many sailors at church that morning. I'm sure most were at home on leave. Following Mass a couple of guys and I walked to chow for a great Christmas breakfast. I spent a quiet Christmas in 1957. The barracks were rather sparse of people this day. I called my dad and wished him and his wife a Merry Christmas. My mother was living in California with my sister. I called them and wished them a Merry Christmas. She was concerned about what I was going to do on Christmas. I told her I was working and was OK. I was looking forward to New Year's Eve as my buddy Bob had a New Years party lined up and I had a couple of bottles of champagne for him and me to drink. It was quiet at Patuxent River that Christmas week. We worked in the radio shop. There wasn't much to do except clean up the paper work and work on some faulty equipment. New Year's Eve couldn't come soon enough. The New Years Party I looked forward to was a bust. My date that night was a naïve Jewish girl who served egg nog to drink and wouldn't kiss anyone at midnight. Bob and I drank our champagne and were slightly tipsy. Happy Near Year 1958!!!!!!!

Chapter 11

The Pax River Routine

After the holidays the squadron settled into a normal routine. We worked in the shop, flew test hops, ate, went on Liberty and repeated week after week. The base was located about fifty seven miles from Washington D.C. Many of us took trips to visit the nation's capitol as tourists. In addition there were a lot of single women to meet and have fun with.

One Saturday afternoon in January Bob Biss asked me, "Bruce, would you like to meet some local girls tonight?"

I responded quicker than I thought I could, "I sure would. Where did you meet them and who are they?"

"Well Tom and I went out checking out the area last week and met them at the local drive in. We went inside to order rather than sit in the car to eat and they were sitting at a table having a burger and a Coke. We introduced ourselves and talked to them. One of them is named Sara and the other is named Paula. They were very friendly to us and Sara invited us to her house tonight to visit. Tommy is standing a watch, so I thought I would ask you."

"Thanks for inviting me. Tommy's bad luck is my good luck. When are we leaving?" I asked.
I still had on my dungarees from work. "How much time do we have?" I asked Bob.

"Not much," he retorted. "Do I have time to shower and shave?"

"You have 15 minutes. Get moving," he let me know. I moved and in 14 minutes I was ready to go.

"Let's hit the road," Bob replied. We were looking forward to a great evening. We met the girls at Sara's house in Leonardtown, Maryland. Bob introduced me to the ladies. After meeting the girls, Sara explained, "Paula and I have been friends since we were little kids in elementary school." I noted quickly that Sara was a dish water blonde with a slight twist in her nose. She was well built and very out going. Paula was a slim tall girl with long black hair and great hips. She also was out going and both girls were very attractive. As we talked about ourselves, Bob settled in with Sara and me with Paula.

Paula told us, "Both of us are seniors at St, Mary's Academy in Leonardtown, Maryland. St. Mary's is an all girls' Catholic school. Our teachers are nuns. Many of the girls are country girls and their parents feel that it is better for us to attend an all girls' school. Sometimes it is a good thing, but we miss being with the boys during the day."

Biss and I just listened and nodded at each other. I thought to myself, Biss and I will fill the gap ladies. It was at that point that we all decided to go out to the local drive-in to get a Coke and a burger. It was a great night having the opportunity to talk with girls rather than sailors. It was getting late, about 2400, and both Bob and I had to fly early in the morning and Sara had to open the local radio station and sing at 0900. Sara told us that she sang gospel songs on WKIK the local radio station every Sunday morning. She played guitar and accompanied herself. We dropped off the girls at Sara's house, said our good byes and as we were walking made dates for the next Friday. Bob kissed Sara good night and I leaned down to kiss Paula. She surprised me by opening her mouth and kissing me soundly. Holy Moses, It had been at least 6 months since I had kissed a girl. My engagement was broken and I was footloose and fancy free. Hopefully this was the start of something new and exciting.

Floyd came back from leave with his new bride. Her name was Jo. Jo had graduated from nurse's training and had received her hat at graduation. I had met Jo when Floyd and I were training at Memphis. She was very happy and Floyd was radiant. They were like two peas in a pod. Bob and I visited them in their new little house which was located in the city of Lexington Park. It was too small for me, but they were both very satisfied. Floyd had found a 1950 Pontiac sedan to drive. It had some problems with the transmission. Floyd found a replacement transmission at the local junk yard. He and I spent one Saturday morning replacing the transmission. It ran like a dream after we fixed the problem.

It was January 1958 and the weather had turned to Maryland winter weather. It was cold and dreary. It seemed to rain almost every day. Wet and blustery was the way we explained it. But things were going well with the girls and Bob and I were happy working and flying.

We all mustered in at the normal time of 0700. The day started as any other with coffee and conversation about Dick Clark and bandstand and who went to Washington and what women they met. Bob was scheduled to fly January 10th but had a doctor's appointment that day and told the Chief that he needed someone to replace him. The Chief told him that they were going to be flying that day in the Squadrons cargo aircraft. It was a R7V Super Constellation that looked like a real airplane rather that a WV. He asked anyone in the shop that morning if they had flown in this aircraft before. I'm not sure anyone had. Our buddy Larry Rudder volunteered to replace Bob. He thought it would be a good experience to fly in this aircraft and that it was a quiet day in the shop. "The plane was in pre-flight so you better get moving," said the Chief. The plane was scheduled for a 0715 takeoff. Larry took off running.

It was 0845 when someone from the OD office came into the radio shop and announced that the R7V that was flying training hops this morning had crashed into the woods at the end of the runway. He didn't have any other information at that time. We in the shop looked at the Chief and he strongly suggested that we get out there and help do whatever necessary. One of the guys had a car that we all jumped into and headed out to the field. By the time we got there the base fire trucks were there and rescue people from the base were on the scene. We told the personnel who were in charge who we were and that we wanted to help if possible. They told us there was nothing we could do. There were no survivors. They would advise the squadron of the next steps to take. We went back to the shop in tears. Our friend Larry Rudder had died along with a number of VW-11 shipmates. It was a sad day for VW-11.

Larry's best friend Dick Judy took Larry's remains home to his family and fiancée. I'm sure it was a very difficult trip for Dick as he was to be Larry's best man in June. It was a difficult week for us all. There was a special service at chapel for all of those who were lost. There was an overflow attendance at the service. I think Bob was the saddest of all as Larry was flying for him. We assured him that the Lord works in many ways and it was not his time or his fault. This provided little consolation at the time. I needed to get Bob out and get him back to positive thinking again. We were scheduled to go out with the girls that weekend. Hopefully this would help.

We went dancing. The girls knew of a place called Tall Timbers located back in the woods down toward Cedar Point. It was a bar with a good sized dance floor. They had a band in from Washington D.C. that night. We found out that the girls were seventeen but that Paula enjoyed drinking beer and Sara liked white wine. We were surprised that the waitress didn't question us or the ladies regarding our ages. So we danced and drank all evening. It was a fun night and all the way home Paula and I necked in the back seat of Bob's car. I felt sorry for Bob as I was enjoying the ride in the back seat.

Over the next months my relationship with Paula grew more serious. Bob and Sara were together a lot also. The four of us really enjoyed each other's company. One warm March evening of dancing at Tall Timbers, we were all soaking wet from the exercise. A little wine and beer made us feel adventuresome. I asked Paula, "Where can we take a quick dip in the river to cool down?" She looked at me and said "We don't have any bathing suits to put on." Being adventuresome I looked at her, Bob, and Sara and blurted out, "Why do we need bathing suits? Let's go skinny dipping!"

"We can go to the pipeline. There is a quiet private beach there. It's too late for anyone to be there and, with the exception of a security light or two it will be dark," Sara noted. Bob and I agreed, but Paula and Sara both said they would go if Bob and I would cover our eyes while they were getting into the water. That was an easy decision for Bob and me to make. Off we went to the beach. The girls left the car to take off their clothes behind a stand of trees and Bob and I took ours off in the car and headed to the river. We got into the water and rinsed off. The water was cool but not cold. The girls shouted, "Turn around. Here we come. How's the water? Where are you guys?" "Ok, we'll turn around and the water is cool but not cold."

In they came. When they reached the water we turned around and watched as they tiptoed into the river. What a beautiful sight, the two young women with the moon coming up behind them as they entered the water. It was probably the first time anyone other that their mothers had seen them naked since they were babies. "You guys weren't supposed to be looking," they shouted. "We can't see anything its. It's too dark. Rinse yourselves off. It feels good to cool down." We followed them back into the water and started a water splashing fight with the girls. We had a lot of fun that evening. Bob left the heater going in the car so that we will be able to warm up and dry off. Hell, we didn't have any towels. We would figure that out, after all we were sailors and should be able to fix that oversight. We did. The girls used their slips and we our undershirts. It was a great night that we all talked about many times after that.

As the months of January, February, and early March wore on the routine continued: flying and working, seeing the girls, spending time visiting my friends in Washington. Life was good and I was working to achieve my next rank, third-class petty officer. Paula and Sara invited Bob and me to their high school prom. We were looking forward to that.

During early March 1958 the VW-11 Squadron was advised that it was deploying back to Argentia and would be permanently home ported there in early April. That was a shock to the whole squadron. We were told that the reason VW-11 was picked was because we were the most efficient operationally from both the flying and the maintenance perspective. Wasn't that exciting? The married folks were very concerned about what was going to happen to their families. Families would be moved to Argentia as soon as housing was completed during the summer of 1958. Chiefs, 1st class petty officers, and 2nd class petty officers would move in that order as housing would be completed. Captains, Commanders, LT. Commanders, LTs. and LT. JGs in that order would move in as housing was completed. It would be a logistics nightmare, but would be worked out. Details would be passed along as required.

All the plans of mice and men were changed. The single guys, non-commissioned officers, and airmen would be moved into crew quarters and barracks. The single officers would be moved into the Bachelor Officer Quarters.

When the announcement was made we knew what we had to do. We had bad news for the girls. No more good times, no more dancing, no more double dates, and no Prom. I'm sure they would not be happy with the U. S. Navy. Bob and I certainly weren't.

We had about three more weeks left before we were going to leave for Argentia. It was Easter weekend. Paula invited me to spend the day with her and her family. I hadn't broken the news to her yet, but I'm sure she had heard the rumors. Things like that in a Navy community get around rather quickly. Easter in 1958 was in the middle of March. We had a wonderful day. We went to church together and I met the whole family: mom, dad, two sisters and a brother. Paula was the youngest of the group. What a nice day, I found out that one of her sisters was married to a Navy Chief that was part of the ship's company at Patuxent River. Her mother was concerned that Paula was dating a sailor. I tried to assure her that I was a nice sailor and had good intentions. I don't think she was sure that was true. Dinner was great with all the Easter trimmings.

But I had to let Paula know that VW-11 was leaving. After lunch we took a walk down to the river. While walking I put my arm around her and told her the bad news. "Paula, VW-11 is moving to Argentia in April this year," I noted. We don't have much time left together before I will be leaving. Going to the prom and your graduation will not happen for me and you."

"I heard, honey," she replied. "One of the girls at school whose dad is in VW-11 told Sara and me the bad news. We will just have to make do. It won't be the same without you and Bob going to the prom with us. It has been a wonderful three months. I'm sure my mother will be happy." I thought to myself what a practical way to look at bad news.

"We will just have a great two or three weeks together before I have to go." We spent all of my time off together during that period and the relationship deepened. She was getting ready to graduate and I was getting ready to leave.

During the busy schedule we had getting ready to move the radio shop we were advised by the Chief that there would be a new lineup of flight crews once we reached Argentia. Crews would be assigned in the same living quarters. That is, all the single men in each crew would have their own crew room to live in. The non flight crew enlisted men would be assigned to living in a barracks type atmosphere. The Chief had put together radio operators in pairs by crew. I was assigned to "25 knothole" as a radioman. The other radioman would be Randal Speak.

The last night Paula and I were together was very sad and teary. I borrowed Floyd's Pontiac. We went out to dinner at a fish house down in Cedar Point and didn't talk about my leaving during dinner. We talked about all the fun we had the past months. Following dinner we drove down to the river at Sandy Bottom and got into the back seat. We fell into each others arms and didn't let go for hours. We talked about us, the future, and what we could do about it. The "m" word didn't come up, as we thought that we were too young to even give it thought. We didn't make love, but came close to it a number of times. Paula wanted to remain a virgin. Of course I honored her decision. As I dropped her off that night we agreed that we loved each other and would write every day. I headed home to the barracks, a sad fellow that night.

It was on April 15, 1958 that VW-11 began its departure for Argentia. This would be home port for the next 9 years.

Chapter 12

The Crew
25 knothole

The Officers:

Willy Victor crews were made up of 21 or 22 personnel. Normally, the make up included 3 pilots; a plane commander, 2nd and 3rd pilots with the third pilot being in training. There were two flight engineers, one electrician who doubled as cook, two navigators, two radio operators, two radar technicians, two CIC officers and 5-7 CIC terminal operators. Crew 25 knothole was typical. The personnel were all individuals. The officers of the crew were the pilots, navigators, and the CIC officers. The remainder of the crew was enlisted. With the exception of the flight engineers the enlisted crew members were mostly kids. By that I mean, under 21 years of age.

Our plane commander was LTC Fox. He had over 20,000 flying hours. He was the plane commander in VW-11 with the most flying hours. He began his career in the Navy during World War II. Many of his flying hours were in PBY aircraft. PBY aircraft were used as long range patrol planes and for saving downed fighter pilots and flight crew members on the Pacific front during the war. He was an outstanding pilot and Naval Officer during his time in the Pacific. One of the aircraft he was flying made a disastrous landing in rough seas on one engine. The aircraft flipped upside down upon hitting a very high wave. Commander Fox sustained a broken back during the crash, but he and all of his crew were rescued. He recovered from the injuries and continued his career as a pilot, no doubt with pain as he couldn't bend over easily. He was highly decorated and retired from the Navy with honors. All of us in the 25 knothole crew felt we were the luckiest crew in VW-11 having LTC Fox as our Plane Commander and would go through hell with and for him.

LTJG Robert Book was our 2nd pilot. The enlisted guys called him "Bookie". He was from the state of Kansas. He went to Kansas University and joined the Navy to fly. He had about 6 years in the Navy when he was assigned to VW-11. He had about 1000 hours of flight time to his credit. He was a good pilot and was well liked by the crew. He invited the enlisted portion of the crew to his home for dinner. He was married and had 1 child. His wife was very beautiful. We thought he was a very lucky man.

Our third pilot Ensign Jack Stahl came to us from the Navy's multi-engine flight school. He had about 200 hours of flying under his belt. He also served as our third navigator. We always knew when he was landing the aircraft. We always hit the runway hard. We knew that LTC Box was in the right seat when he was flying. He was a University Of Michigan graduate and joined the Navy to fly. We, the enlisted liked him. He had about two years in the Navy when he was assigned to VW-11. He was single and lived in the BOQ (Bachelor Officer Quarters). He set up the bowling competition between the enlisted members of 25 knothole and the officers.

We had two CIC Officers, LTJG Glen Plover and Ensign Bill Peach. Both were Graduates of the Navy's CIC Officers Training School at NAS Glynco, Georgia and following graduation in late 1956 were transferred to VW-11 at Patuxent, Maryland. Both Plover and Peach came up through the ranks and were well liked by the enlisted crew. These were 30 year men. That is they were going to serve at least 30 years in the Navy before retirement.

Our first Navigator was LTJG Pete Bankowski. We all thought he was the best navigator in the squadron. But, he was all business and didn't associate much with the enlisted crew. He graduated from the Academy in 1955 wanted to fly, but washed out of flight school because of a physical problem. We never knew what that was. He knew everything about navigation there was to know. He used all techniques. I watched him shoot the sun, the stars, use the radar, the loran, and dead reckon. Most of the other navigators we had never tried the stars, sun, or the Loran to navigate for us while flying the barrier.

Our second navigator was Ensign Rick Nafis. He was the enlisted crew's best friend. He graduated from the ROTC program at Rutgers in 1955. Following Officers Candidate School, he went to the Navy's navigator training center in Pensacola, Florida, graduated at the bottom of his class and was assigned to VW-11 in 1956. He was ok as a navigator but wasn't too sure about shooting the stars, sun or using Loran. He always used the radar or received fixes from the picket ships on the barrier, or used dead reckoning. This caused us some problems during his tenure. We all thought that the Ensign was the highest rank he would achieve during his time in the Navy. He always looked out for us (the enlisted crew). Whenever we landed in the Azores, he would hand out penicillin pills to the enlisted guys should they hook up with the local ladies.

The Enlisted Crew:

The electrician in our crew was Electrician first class Jack Bannister. Jack was a great guy and was working toward retirement. When he came to VW-11 he had 11 years with the Navy. His previous experience flying was with a VP squadron out of NAS Quonset Point, Rhode Island. The electrician's role in the crew was two-fold. First he was responsible for all the wiring in the A/C as well as the Auto-pilot equipment. This was a complex piece of equipment that allowed the plane to be flown on auto-pilot, very critical to pilots as they could put the plane on auto pilot for the long hours of flying we did. If the equipment failed, the pilots would have to fly the plane manually for hours. This was very labor intensive and tiresome. His second role, the one the crew felt was his most important, was the cook. Jack did a great job as cook. We never ever were not satisfied by his effort. His efforts on Easter and Christmas we thought rivaled our mothers. Jack was married and lived in the new enlisted married quarters. We never had the opportunity to meet his wife.

We had two flight engineers. One was Andy Harder and the other was Bill Murphy. Both were First Class Aviation Machinist Mates. Both were married, had families, and lived in the new enlisted married quarters. Both Andy and Bill came up through the enlisted rank as aircraft mechanics and plane Captains. Both attended flight engineers and plane training at the Lockheed Corporation Super Constellation training center in Los Angeles prior to being assigned to VW-11 in late 1956. One thing we all knew was that both of our Flight Engineers were well versed in the Super Connie we were flying and could take it apart and put it back together again if needed. That was very reassuring to both the enlisted crew as well as the officers. Andy came up with leather wallets he made by hand for the squadron's various knothole crews and sold them to all who wanted one. The price for each wallet was six dollars and provided each individual crew with their own crew wallet. The wallets were hand made by Andy. I'm sure he also made a buck or two on each one. He professed that he wasn't making them just for his own benefit. Most of the 25 knothole crew bought one.

We had two radio operators. Our responsibilities included all of the radio equipment in the WV we were flying as well as providing Morse code communications with NWP7, whom we communicated with while flying via low frequency radio bands. You already know who I am but the other radio operator was Randal Speak. Randal was a good ole boy from Ravenswood, North Carolina. Until he joined the Navy, Randal never traveled out of the state. He was very interested in cars as his daddy was a moonshiner and made the finest moonshine in the state. Randal was proud to let everyone know that he was the mechanic on his dad's car before he joined the Navy. In fact, Randal said that the reason he joined the Navy was to get away from home as quick as he could so he would not get caught by the federal agents who were onto his daddy. He decided to become an Aviation Electronics Technician to learn a trade other than car mechanics. He did have aspirations to be a mechanic on a racing team. We never knew if he made it or not. Randal and I flew together until I left Argentia in August of 1959. Randal was a real down to earth person and would give you the shirt off of his back if necessary. When I left the squadron, he was dating a Newfie lady named Christie. She and Randal seemed like "peas and carrots", as an 1980's philosopher, Forrest Gump, once said of things that go well together.

There were two radar technicians on our crew. They were responsible for the operation of the two radars the Super Connie carried. One was the APS 20 long range search radar and the APS 90 height finding radar. Our technicians were Aubrey Smith and Jack Buckman. What a pair they were. Aubrey was an Aviation Electronics Technician 3rd class and Jack was an Aviation Electronics Technician 2nd class. Aubrey was a 5 foot 6 inch banty rooster from Pecos, Texas. He chose the service in 1956 rather than going to jail for drunkenness and fighting. Aubrey obviously chose the Navy and picked electronics to learn so he would have a way to get a job after his service time was completed. He was a proud Texan and would fight with anyone to prove it, particularly when drunk on bourbon. He would wear his cowboy boots anytime he could. He wore them especially when we were flying. He always said if the plane crashed he wanted to die with his boots on. If one of the officers caught him they would make him take them off. That happened a lot, so he always brought his Navy broughams with him to replace them when he was caught wearing them.

Jack Buckman was from Erie, Pennsylvania. He was a big guy, about 6 feet 2 inches or 3 inches tall and was a high school basketball hero. He was loud and liked to brag about his prowess. He told us he was looking for a scholarship his senior year, but none came. That was very disappointing for Jack as he thought because of his success in high school one would come. The scholarship never arrived. He was unhappy with his coach as he was told one was imminent. His Dad had no money to send him to school. He had no other options but to get drafted, so he joined the Navy. Jack turned 21 in 1959. He celebrated that every weekend at the Petty officer club until I left the squadron. He started seeing a very attractive Newfie named Steffie while I was there. He married her sometime in 1960. When he left the service he returned to York, Pennsylvania, opened a hardware store and married Steffie and they lived the American dream. Both Jack and Aubrey played on the squadron basketball team.

We had 9 CIC ACW enlisted in our crew. What a group they were. All of them under 21 like most of us. There was Larry Standrich, Harry Mellow, Frank Jericho, Don Burgois, Dave Spring, Celso Ramirez, Jim Giovanetti, Luke Flanders, and Fred "Teenbeat" Landrow.

Larry was a kid form Des Moines, Iowa. He was one of the three short guys we called the three musketeers. He was the first one. He joined the Navy to see the world. Following his time in the service Larry became an air controller working for the FAA in Louisville, Kentucky. The second musketeer was Frank Justin. He was from Minneapolis, Minnesota. He wasn't ready to join the railroad yet, so he joined the Navy, like Larry, to see the world. When his time in the service was completed Frank went back to Minnesota and joined the railroad, got married and with his wonderful wife fathered and raised 8 children. Finally, the third Musketeer was Don Burgois. His nickname was Baggage. He was from the Massachusetts area, and loved music. He collected all the popular records during his time in Argentia, shared them with all of us and his brown bagger friends. Don married when he left the service and worked for the post office until retirement. My family had an opportunity to meet Don and his family in 1971. My children noticed immediately that he had a very close resemblance to the famous Sonny Bono of Sonny and Cher fame. All three of the musketeers met in ACW training at Glen Coe, Georgia. What a group they turned out to be. They shared a lot of experiences together before they joined the crew including their women, at least in Newfoundland.

Dave Spring was the youngest of the ACW crew. He came from Rhode Island. He always was longing for his girlfriend. She apparently longed for him also as she sent him pairs of her panties and some of her pubic hairs that he smelled all the time and always carried a pair with him when he was flying. We all wanted a smell but, he would never let us. We kidded him a lot. He finally married the girl and lived in one room they rented in Placentia, outside the base. I never did find out how long that lasted as I left Argentia in August of 1959.

Celso Ramirez was of Mexican heritage and came from Laredo Texas. Laredo was just across the Rio Grand River from Neuebo, Laredo Mexico. Where after a period of time we found out that Celso spent a lot of time there in his youth in Mexico across the river. In fact, whenever he went home on leave he would spend one day initially at home 12 days in a Mexican house of ill repute across the river, one day at home and then back to Argentia. He was always tired when he got back. He would always sleep about two days when he returned. Celso joined the Navy to see the world but also to get an education as the opportunities for a Mexican kid in Laredo weren't very good.

Jim Giovanetti was an Italian kid from Boston. He grew up in the North End with his parents who emigrated from Italy in 1915 and owned a restaurant. He loved to have fun and was a practical joker. He was always pulling stunts on the three musketeers. He smoked like a fiend. He and Harry always vied for the position of who was going to have the first cigarette in the morning. We always thought that he would burn down the barracks with his smoldering cigarettes.

Luke Flanders was an Irish kid from Kansas City. He had a great personality, but had an ever present chip on his shoulder. He was slight of build, but always wanted to fight. When he drank too much he always wanted to fight with Jim. Apparently, he had something for Italians and was always looking to Jim to fulfill his need. They were great friends when sober. Luke's family was working class folks. His dad worked in the flour mills and his mom raised the five kids. He had two brothers and two sisters. The girls were beautiful and had red hair and green eyes. All of us in the crew wanted to go home with him to meet his sisters. He told us he wouldn't trust us with his sisters. We all wanted to meet them. We never got the opportunity.

Fred (teen beat) Landrow was a character. He loved music and was singing all the time. Between Burrgois and him we had all the popular music of the time playing in the barracks. Teenbeat and Burrgois managed to find a lot of antenna cable and strung it outside of our barracks room. They tuned into a radio station from Boston, Massachusetts so that they could get the latest rock and roll music for the crew. Teenbeat was a typical kid from the Bronx, wise cracking and always up to date on the latest gouge and rumors. He walked with a beat and a loud confidence. His shoes were always shined as he said like a "Niggers Heel". Being from the Bronx he knew what that meant. We sure didn't.

Last but not least was Harry Mellow. He was born and raised in Philadelphia, Pennsylvania. We thought he came from a mafia family in Philadelphia. Harry slept in the upper bunk next to a group of lockers. He placed his cigarettes and ash tray on top of the lockers. This enabled him to have easy access to them in the morning and at night before falling asleep. The first thing Harry did in the morning was to grab a cigarette and light it. The last thing he did at night was to put out his cigarette in the ash tray before he fell asleep. It was a wonder that he didn't start either himself or the barracks on fire. Harry joined the Navy to get an education and determine what he wanted to do with the rest of his life. He had a great personality and was well liked by the rest of the crew. Celso was always after him to quit smoking.

This was the crew, made up of mostly kids doing their service time for the United States of America. We flew together; we lived in the same room with each other, and had fun together. We were not unlike the other crews that flew the barriers in the Atlantic and Pacific. We were Americans doing our part to protect our country. We all had experiences that we would never forget.

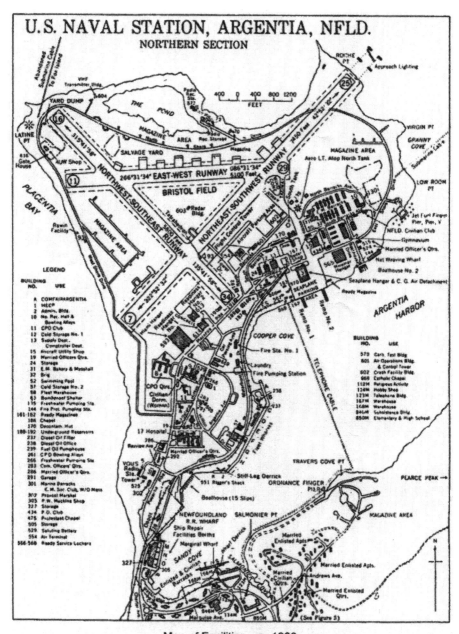

Map of Facilities, ca. 1960

Overhead Map of NAS Argentia

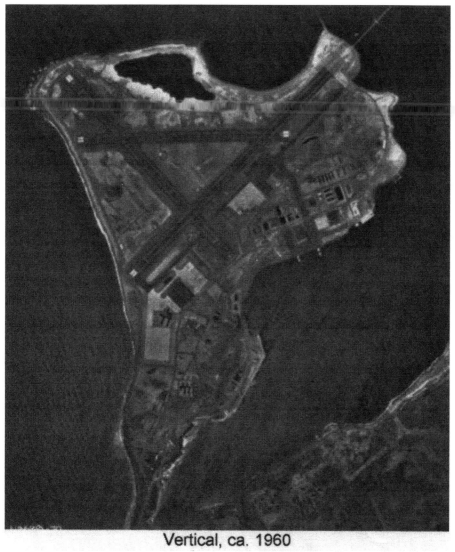

Vertical, ca. 1960

Argentia, Newfoundland from the air

Movie Theater at Argentia

**Low building at left is EM Club at Argentia.
The hill to the barracks.**

WV-2s flying in formation over Pax River

WV-s flying in formation over Chesapeake Bay

WV-2 pilot training flight over Pax River

VW-15 WV-2 on tarmac in Argentia, Newfoundland. Signed by Admiral Finley

WV-2s on tarmac Argentia, Newfoundland

Bruce Jarvis

VW-4 Hurricane Hunter on tarmac at Barbers Point

Coming home from barrier
Landing at Argentia Nfld

MUSEUM WILL HOST
"ALL-SQUADRON"
WILLY VICTOR REUNION

On September 5,6, and 7, 2003, the museum will host a reunion for past Navy veterans that were attached to both Atlantic and Pacific Fleet Airborne Early Warning Squadrons. In the mid 1950s, during the height of the cold war, America, fearing a Soviet Union attack on our East or West Coasts, commissioned 244 "Warning Star" Super Constellations built by Lockheed Aircraft Corporation. The Air Force received seventy-four and the remainder were delivered to the U.S. Navy.

The "Willy-Victor (WV-2) has a maximum flight endurance of thirty hours, carried a crew of twenty-six, and had nearly six tons of radar equipment. The flight crew worked in shifts, and while off duty, the aircraft provided sleeping bunks and a galley to provide hot meals. Thus, for nearly ten years, twenty-four hours per day, seven days a week, the frontiers of the American defense system were patrolled by WV-2 aircraft based in Alaska, Honolulu, Midway, and Argentia, Newfoundland. Due to the invention of land based radar tracking the curvature of the earth, the last airborne radar flight was flown in 1965.

Today, there are only four WV-2 aircraft known to exist. The Octave Chanute Aerospace Museum is proud to boast that it has one of the four, BU No. 141311. The aircraft was delivered to Chanute Air Force Base in 1983. Over the years it was badly neglected as it sat on the flight line becoming home to hundreds of generations of pigeons. In 1999 it was turned over to the museum and in April 2000 ex-Willy-Victor crewmen from across the United States organized work parties to start restoration of the aircraft. After thousands of hours of labor by countless volunteers, "311" looks as good as she did in 1957 when coming off the assembly line and being delivered to Airborne Early Warning Squadron 13, Patuxent River Naval Air Station, Maryland.

The reunion will be an opportunity for all squadron members attending to board the aircraft and relive their memories of long ago. In addition, the reunion plans include admission to the museum, a welcoming buffet on Friday night at the CaddyShack Restaurant, a field trip or a golf outing on Saturday and the reunion banquet on Saturday evening. According to Marty Zvonar, member of the Reunion Committee, at the time of this printing, approximately 500 people are expected to attend.

Willy Victor Reunion 2003

Rantoul, Illinois
Octave Chanute Aerospace Museum

Saturday, September 6, 2003
1800 Hours

Master of Ceremonies .... Marty Zvonar, VW-13
Reunion Committee
Banquet Pre-Entertainment .. N.R.O.T.C. Drill Team
Reid Nannen, Commander
University of Illinois
Presentation of Colors .... Lincoln's Challenge Academy
National Anthem .... Dr. Janice M. Bahr
Professor of Physiology, Animal Sciences
University of Illinois

Please Join in Singing the National Anthem

Address of Welcome .... Honorable Tim Johnson
U.S. House of Representatives
15th District, Illinois
Invocation .... Don Kruse
Past American Legion Department of Illinois Chaplain

Dinner

Introduction of Speaker .... Donald O. Weckhorst
CMSgt U.S.A.F. (Ret.)
Keynote Speaker .... Keith Tedrow
Brigadier General U.S.A.F. (Ret.)
Special Recognition .. Wes Mortenson, AEWBARRON PAC
Chairman, Reunion Committee
Closing Remarks .... Marty Zvonar

A "Very Special Guest"
WV-2 Navy BUNO
141311

♦ Delivered to U.S. Navy -- 10 August 1956
♦ Served in six (6) different Squadrons
♦ Total Airframe Flight-Time -- 12,353 Hours
♦ Retired: 4 June 1983

Three Minute Memories
Immediately following the Banquet, we wish to
extend a welcome to members that may want to "Step-up"
to the microphone and share any "special sea stories"
pertaining to the life of a "Willy-Victor" Sailor that
happened so long ago.

Hotel Wellington, New York City, LASI Trip

Pacific Barrier Crew

AEWRON Squadron Patches

Chapter 13

25 knothole Settling In

Each flight crew was provided with a crew room. That is all the single enlisted men of the crew were billeted in a single room. The rooms were large enough to house 14 personnel. Included in each room were double bunks, a table and chairs and lockers for each man. It was cozy to say the least, but comfortable enough that you weren't running into each other. The purpose of this arrangement was to be able to awaken a crew at all hours and not bother other personnel sleeping in the other rooms. It also provided for the crews to get to be more like a family and create a great working team.

"25 knothole" did just that. We were from various parts of the country and each of us brought his personality and philosophy to the crew. We had a great time together and shared experiences that would last a life time. We ate together, slept together, played together, laughed together, drank together, and were panicked together. One thing we didn't do was share our women. We may have been envious of each other because of the situations we were faced with, but we managed the situations well. We found out early that we all liked women and in most cases the women liked us.

When we first moved into the room we found out that we were all under the age of 21. We spent our drinking time at the EM club down the hill from the barracks. That is until Jack Buckman turned 21 and made 2nd class petty officer. He then transitioned to the petty officer club and drank hard liquor. The highest rate any of us had other than Jack was third class petty officer. Our highest pay grade was E-4 until Jack went to E-5. Our adventure began and continued on until 1962 when the last member of the original crew either left the Navy or was transferred to another command.

Our crew played pinochle. We became experts in the game of two deck pinochle. Following every flight we would shower and start a game of pinochle. These games would last until all hours. Sometimes 4-5 hours in length or until someone who wasn't playing wanted to sleep and wanted the players to quiet down. The players always complained and always stopped playing.

Time off was spent playing basketball, going to the gym on base to work out or play handball, going to the commissary to buy supplies, going bowling, fishing, or visiting friends. I coached the VW-11 squadron basketball team. Jack, and Aubry played on the team. We didn't do too bad. As much as we didn't like them, we respected the Marines. We just couldn't beat the Marines. As the coach I always thought that since the referees were Marines might have been the reason. Conjecture to say the least.

There were nightly movies at the base theater. This was a popular pastime. Many of us when we didn't go to the club attended the movies. The movies were bad and changed every evening, but they weren't class "A" by any means. Most were "B", "C", or "D". I'm convinced that the Navy got them for free and shipped the worst ones to Argentia.

Once in the while a USO group would come to entertain the troops. This was always a big occasion at the base. As I recall the biggest entertainer to visit us during my tenure was Connie Francis. She was very big in the States and gave us a two hour show. She was great and we all loved her, especially Burgois. He being our music and record man, fell in love with her. She is all he talked about for two weeks. I can say the Navy tried to entertain us and keep our morale up.

The brown baggers, the married folks in the squadron who lived on the base invited us to their homes for dinner and some of us to their parties. Many of us babysat for them. There was only one television station on the base. If you were lucky when you babysat and the brown baggers had a television set you could watch it. The programming was not very good, but it was TV. In addition you could make collect calls back home from the phone in the home. Although there was only one telephone circuit to the world from Argentia, it was normally available for long distance calls back to the states late in the evening. One always made sure you reversed the charges for those calls.

I was fortunate to bartend at many Brown bagger parties. By the time the party was over I usually was about as tipsy as the party givers and attendees were. Normally I would then sleep on the party givers' couch that evening. It was a welcome break from pinochle and the guys.

Fishing was another pastime some of us enjoyed. When we would return from barrier flights the plane normally followed the road from St. Johns to Argentia. One of us would look out the porthole of the aircraft and look for lakes located off the road at some point that could be recognized from the ground. We would then go and find the location to fish in. The fishing was great. The lakes all had either rainbow or brown trout in them. Apparently there wasn't enough food to feed all the fish in these lakes. I say this because as soon as the bait hit the water you caught a fish. Stringers would always be full of fresh fish.

During the grunion runs in the spring we would fish off of the shore at the base. The cod fish would attack the grunion and push the schools of them to swim close to the shore. We would bait our spinning rods with pieces of grunion that had run up on the shore and catch stringers full of cod.

Between the trout and cod the brown baggers would have fish fries and invite us to join them for dinner. It was a little bit of home for us and the fish were wonderful eating. The crew had many great experiences both when flying barriers and during the times we had off. Members of the enlisted crews became fast friends forever.

Chapter 14

Lockheed Air Service

New York, New York

After flying 400 hours each Willy Victor that flew on the Atlantic side of the United States was flown to Lockheed Air Service (LASI) located at Idlewild Airport, in New York City. Each Willy Victor that flew on the Pacific side of the United States was flown to the LASI Service located at Honolulu International airport for the same purpose. Lockheed then would basically tear the entire A/C apart and put it back together again. Initially each VW-11 crew would have an opportunity to fly a Willy Victor that needed service to Lockheed. It was 25 knothole's turn to take a WV-2 to LASI. It was a great opportunity to spend some time in the states, generally one or two nights in the big city. This was our first trip to LASI. The date was April, 20 1959. After about a year and a half of transporting Willy Victors to LASI by individual crews the squadron commander started to allow other VW-11 sailors such as mechanics, personnel men, etc. that would never have a chance for liberty in New York to fly down with the crews and enjoy the city. It was a great morale booster. We had a replacement radioman for this trip as Randal couldn't make the trip. My buddy Bob Biss volunteered to replace Randal for this trip.

One of the first things each of us did was to contact the housewives of the brown baggers that we knew and asked them if there was something that they needed, that they couldn't get at the base commissary, and we could get in New York City for them. One item they all wanted was Pledge furniture polish. Apparently it was a new product that the commissary didn't carry. The commissary at Argentia wasn't prepared for all of the married personnel who were brought to the base in 1958-1959. They had limited products and goods needed by the housewives of Argentia. So we, the young enlisted on the VW-11 flight crews, helped them out when we took our planes to LASI. To say the least they were grateful.

The other Bruce, a buddy of mine, had an uncle in New York City that was a manager of the Hotel Wellington in the city. Bruce gave me his uncle's name and the address and phone number of the hotel he managed. Bruce indicated that his uncle would take care of us, just mention his name. We kept his uncle in mind when we traveled to LASI. We landed at 1000 hours. It was an interesting approach.

At about 0800 the commander Fox contacted Idlewild control to get clearance to land. "Idlewild control this is Navy 141327, request to land."

"Navy 141327, this is Idlewild control. What is your altitude and location?"

"This is Navy 141327. We are at 5000 ft on a course heading 0200 degrees, about 20 miles north of the field."

"Thank you Navy141327. We have you. Please turn left to 090 degrees and climb to 10000 feet. We are very busy and you will have to take your place in line, this is Idlewild control."

"Idlewild control, this is Navy 141327. I have a group of sailors with me going on leave or on liberty and they can't wait in line."

The Commander Fox turned to the flight engineer, "Andy, we are having problems with number four engine, aren't we?"

"Yes, sir," replied Andy who understood what the Commander Fox meant. Shall we feather it, sir?" he asked, "Feather it, Andy." the Commander replied, and the engine was immediately feathered.

"Idlewild Control this is Navy 141327. We have lost our number 4 engine and have feathered it. Request emergency landing instructions to Idlewild airport."

"Navy 141327, will you require emergency equipment on standby for your landing?"

"Yes, please have them standby," replied the commander. "Once we land we will let you know if we need them."

"Navy 141327, you are cleared for an emergency landing on runway 6. Turn right to heading 185 degrees." LCDR Fox greased the landing.

After we landed safely, Andy restarted engine 4 and we headed to LASI. "Idlewild control thank you this is Navy 141327 we will not require emergency equipment. Request ground clearance to Lockheed Air Service."

"Navy 141327 this is Idlewild control you are cleared to LASI."

Once we arrived at LASI and the engines were shut down, Commander Fox let us know what was happening. We gathered forward in the airplane and listened.

"Gentlemen," he started, "I want you all to enjoy your stay, but I want to make sure you all understand that you are to be back here tomorrow at 1200 hours sharp, as we are scheduled to take off at 1400 hours sharp. I'm visiting my wife's relatives on Long Island. Phone number is Michigan that is MI-4635. Mr. Book is staying with his dad and can be reached at Navahoe NA-5689. If you need us, call us. Mr. Book and I do not expect to be called. Have a great liberty. Those of you who are going on leave enjoy your leave and get back to Argentia on time. See you liberty hounds at 1200 hours tomorrow."

Although we had less than 24 hours we were going to enjoy it. Crew 25 knothole was here. The first thing I did when we arrived at LASI after Commander Fox talked to us and we deplaned was to call the hotel to make a reservation and set up a meeting with Bruce Hursey's uncle. He told me to see him when we arrived at the hotel. Bruce was named after his uncle.

Aubrey, Jack, Bob, and I were headed for the hotel and a great night. We grabbed a cab and announced that we wanted to go to Hotel Wellington in Manhattan. When we arrived at the hotel I went to the desk and asked for Mr. Bruce Hursey, who was the hotel manager. The desk clerk was very alert and asked us to please wait. Mr. Hursey came out of the office behind the counter and introduced himself to us. I introduced myself and the others to Mr. Hursey. He was very gracious. "Thank you for calling me and coming down to see me. When I heard that you were friends of my nephew, Bruce, I knew that I wanted to meet you all and help you if I could."

"George," he called to the bellman. "Take the gentleman to the Washington suite. Fellows, I have a suite with four beds and two bathrooms, if that is ok with all of you."

Unanimously we answered, "Yes, sir. Thank you very much."

"I'm going to comp the room. You will not have to pay for it. It is on the house. You boys enjoy your stay in the city and have a great time," he explained. "Enjoy," he continued as he shook our hands, and told George to help us to the room. "If there is anything else I can do for you, call me directly or call George."

We all thanked Mr. Hursey profusely and followed George to the 15th floor and the Washington suite. George opened the double doors and all we could say was "Wow!!!!!!" The doors opened to a large room with couches, chairs, lamps, and tables spread out with a large bay window looking out on the city. The room was decorated in blues, grays, and matching red colors with curtains that opened and closed automatically. George showed us the bar with a refrigerator and ice maker. He opened the refrigerator and it was loaded with Budweiser and Miller beer. He then took us to the door at the left of the room, opened it and there were twin beds and a door to the bathroom. We were in awe with our eyes open wide and tongues hanging out. He took us to the other side of the room, opened the door and we saw the same thing; twin beds and a door to the bathroom. We thanked George, collected a buck from each of us and gave it to George as he left the room with a wink and a smile, saying "Boys, enjoy the big city. Call me if you need anything tonight." Bob and I shared a bedroom and Jack and Aubrey shared the other bedroom.

We looked at each other and yelled out loud. "How lucky we are," said Jack as he sat in a chair. "Lets get a beer and figure out where we're going tonight," said Aubrey. He walked over to the refrigerator and took out four beers and opened them. "Anyone want ice?" We all busted out laughing and enjoyed the beer. "Wait until I tell Bruce about his uncle's hospitality," I shouted. Bob then informed us, "I know of a great Jazz bar down on Times Square. All of the best Jazz stars play there until 0300 or 0400 every day. It is the greatest." We all looked at each other and agreed that this place would be a great place to start.

The New York drinking age in those days was eighteen and we were going to have a ball. We all took a shower, put on some civilian clothes and took the elevator to the lobby, walked out of the hotel and took the first cab in line outside the hotel and said, "Take us to the Birdland Club on Times Square." The cabbie said, "Yes, sir," and we were on our way. It took about 20 minutes to get to the Birdland. Traffic was rather heavy. The cabbie announced that the fare was 5 bucks. We gave him seven and left the cab to an unbelievable Times Square with its lights flashing, people rushing somewhere and everywhere, and us going to the Birdland.

A group of about six guys were up behind the bar playing their hearts out. Here we are, four young sailors going into one of the most famous jazz clubs in the world and it was our oyster. Wow! Jack ordered a Tom Collins, Aubrey ordered a beer, Bob ordered a seven seven and I ordered a Tom Collins. "Aubrey, you damn Texan, a beer in New York," said Jack. "Who do you think you are drinking a Tom Collins, shit Pennsylvania puke," said Aubrey.

We started the kidding and sarcasm quickly and we all commented on who was drinking and what they were drinking. After about 3 drinks and lot of conversation with the bartender, Lester, we finally asked him where we should get something to eat, and what we should do to have some fun. Lester was a great guy and seemed to know what he was talking about when he suggested that we go across the street and have dinner at Jack Dempsey's restaurant.

"Who is that guy?" asked Aubrey.

Lester almost flipped, "Hey, man, you don't know who Jack Dempsey is? He was the world champ man, the best there was until Joe Louis came along."

"Who is that guy?" asked Aubrey again.

"Aubrey, you don't know who Joe Louis is?" said Bob.

"That is probably right," said Jack. "Remember, he is from a small podunk town in Texas. They only know about cows and oil. He still has dust in his ears.

I laughed so hard I almost peed my pants, and our buddy, Aubrey, had this sheepish grin on his face. Lester then began to tell Aubrey the Jack Dempsey story and a long tale about Joe Louis.

When he finished all Aubrey could say was, "Well, I'll be damned." Lester said the food was good at Dempsey's restaurant and the best place to have some fun would be in Greenwich Village. He said any cab driver could get us there. We paid the bill and left Birdland a little tipsy. We were going to Jack Dempsey's for dinner. We all ordered T-bone steaks with baked potatoes garnished with butter, sour cream, creamed corn, salad, and apple pie with ice cream. Did we chow down as we only had a box lunch on the airplane hours ago.

Jack Dempsey came over and introduced himself to us. He was a big man with broad shoulders. He was interested in who we were and what we were doing in the city that evening. Jack took the time to explain the situation and Mr. Dempsey didn't charge us for dessert. He said he was very impressed and told us to have a great time. After he left us Aubrey said, "How could he be the world champ? I could take him!"

We all laughed out loud and Bob told Aubrey, "Uh Huh. You couldn't take a flea, let alone Jack Dempsey." We asked our waiter Walter where we should visit in the Village. During dinner Jack thought Walter was a little light in the loafers, but we didn't say anything. He did a good job for us.

Walter suggested about 6 different clubs, but he thought the most fun would be at a bar and club where the show was made up of female impersonators. By the time Walter finished giving us all the glorious details; we had a couple more drinks and were feeling great. We left the restaurant and grabbed a cab to the Club Indigo. It apparently was a popular place as the cabbie knew exactly where it was. As we were leaving the cab, the cabbie told us to watch our wallets, and pay attention to the tab. But, he also said we would have a great time.

The Club Indigo was dark as we entered. On the left was the bar; on the right was the table section in two levels with a stage at the far end. There were a lot of people for a week night and the waiters were very busy serving drinks. The host who was going to seat us said there was a $5 cover charge. We hesitated, but finally his persistence paid off and we gave him the $5 for each of us. We ordered drinks. They all came in fancy glasses, even Aubrey's beer came in a glass. He was impressed. The band started playing Sousa marches as an interlude and after five minutes and a loud flourish out comes the Master of Ceremony. He was some guy dressed like an overweight woman in a pink long dress with pink ostrich feathers sewed around the neck of the dress. He had make-up on over a two day beard and a hairy chest. His hair was a blonde beehive wig. What a sight he was. The audience cheered and shouted as he started his monologue.

I thought Aubrey was going to die. "Where am I? What am I doing here? Who is that queer? Get me out of here." We ordered him another beer and he settled down. The show was made up of various chorus line reviews, all made up of men dressed as women. Some of the women were actually beautiful.

The music was ok and the voices weren't bad. The dancing left something to be desired, but they tried very hard to please the audience. During the show Bob and Jack left the table to make a pit stop and visit the bar. Actually, they went to talk to the MC during the break and asked if he could get one of the impersonators to visit our table and make out with Aubrey. What happened next was one of the most hilarious times of our visit. During the show we had had about 4 or 5 drinks each. We were feeling no pain.

Aubrey was having a great time as we all were. The folks that told us we would enjoy ourselves at this joint were right. It was about 2300 hours when a woman approached our table. She was about 5 feet 8 inches tall in her heels, had long red hair, and was wearing a black low cut shirt to the knees dress. She had on perfect light make-up and was wearing Joy perfume. As she came closer we all swallowed hard. Wow, she was a knock out. Her voice was mid ranged and very sexy. As she came closer she introduced herself, "Hello, my name is Carol. I'm from Loveland, Texas. I understand that you all are from the Navy enjoying the city and the show." We all introduced ourselves to her and told her where we were from. When she reached Aubrey and he said he was from Texas she just swooned over him. Jack, Bob, and I just watched. Unknown to me Jack and Bob set this all up with the MC. The MC thought this stunt was the greatest he had ever heard. Carol thought it would be great to put Aubrey on.

Aubrey's eyes were wide open. He looked at us and said, "I can't believe this is happening." He and Carol were talking like a couple of birds and kids. The show was going on, but Aubrey and Carol were oblivious. As time went on Aubrey started to kiss Carol, first on the cheek and then on the neck and on and on. It was obvious to us that this was going a little too far, and it was getting time to go back to the hotel. Aubrey was having none of it. "You guys go back to the hotel. I'm staying with Carol for a while more." He had continued to drink and was getting silly as heck.

Finally, Carol told Aubrey that she had to go on stage and finish the show. In about 5 minutes Carol was announced to close the show. She closed with "My Funny Valentine". She was stunning in the lights on stage. Aubrey told us he was in love and was going to write to Carol when he got back. We were up standing clapping for the performers when they all took off their hair. We were stunned that this red head was really a man. The most stunned was Aubrey. He couldn't believe it. He looked at us and saw us laughing so large that it finally dawned on him that he had been set up. He threw his beer at us and started hitting us with his program. "You guys set me up. Man, what a women, I thought. I'll get you guys one of these days," Aubrey said with a disappointed look on his face.

It was great night. As we headed back to the hotel in the cab, we all agreed that it had been a great evening. Even Aubrey admitted he had a great evening. We got back to the hotel at 0100 and hit the sack. Reveille was at 0630. Then back to LASI. We had to pick up the brown baggers' requests and get back to the plane we were picking up by 1200 hours. We wanted to have a great civilian breakfast, make a phone call home and shop before we got back to LASI.

As we left the Idlewild runway I looked out my porthole and said good bye for a while to the greatest city in the world and the good ole United States of America until the next time. Sure enough Argentia, Newfoundland welcomed us back to normal with a foggy and rainy GCA landing.

Chapter 15

A Fun Day

Floyd was assigned to be the watch commander. He was responsible for assigning watches to those of us attending training at Norman. His orders were to make sure everyone stood watches. His benefit as watch commander was that he did not have to stand any watches. The watches at Norman were 4 hours in length, a waste of time and at night a waste of our sleep time. We found out that during the winter at Norman it was cold and lonely standing a watch. The typical watch was outside away from any barracks and consisted of walking around old Navy aircraft that were used as part of the training. While standing your watch you were supposed to keep walking around the planes and make sure no one entered the base to steal them or any equipment that was left on them. I was happy to be Floyd's buddy and only stood one watch while at Norman. Floyd Ivy and I became fast friends while at Norman. We would be together for the rest of my time in the service.

It was during the summer of 1958 and a beautiful day in Argentia. Floyd Ivy, his wife, Jo, and, and I decided to go fishing. Jo and Floyd lived in a small one bedroom trailer just outside of Placentia, Newfoundland. I had spent the previous evening playing cards with them. We decided to go fishing the next day, so they asked me so spend the night at their trailer. This would enable us to get an early start as I had to fly that the next evening at 2000 hours. I slept on the couch in my skivvies. Jo provided a pillow and blanket. I had learned that I could sleep just about anywhere after sleeping in the radioman's bunk on the Willy Victor.

When we woke up I made coffee, Jo made breakfast, and Floyd took out the dog. Jo was a good cook. She made eggs, bacon, hash browns and fresh biscuits. Wow, was it great! Jo said, "I'm going to take a cast iron skillet, some Crisco and a bag of flour and herbs to fry the fish you and Floyd catch."

"Sounds interesting to me, but where do we get a fire for you to cook on?" I asked.

"We'll start one on the beach around the lake. As you and Floyd catch the fish, you'll throw them to me, I will take off their heads, gut them, throw them into the flour mixture, then into the skillet that has Crisco in it and we'll eat them like French fries," she added.

She had a plan. Who was I to question it? That sounded good to me. Floyd came back from his walk, finished breakfast and started to get the fishing gear. "Where are we headed Floyd?" I asked.

"I thought we would head down the road toward St. Johns about 2 miles. I spotted a lake about ½ mile walk from the road the last time I flew over it. It looked pristine. Should be great fishing."

"Ok, but I have only the clothes I have on. I didn't bring any others with me last night as I hadn't anticipated staying over," I noted to Floyd.

"Don't worry about it. We'll strip down to our skivvies to fish in. Don't worry about Jo seeing you in your skivvies. You are too good of a friend for that to bother her or me. Hell, as a nurse she has seen a lot of men naked in the operating room," Floyd assured me.

"Let's get going. You have to fly tonight. Jo, do we have the bug spray? Remember the black flies are very bad. Get Bruce a long sleeved shirt or something to cover his arms and neck," noted Floyd as we were walking out the door. "I've got it all in the bag Bruce is carrying," said Jo. Out the door we went. Floyd had the old Pontiac he bought in Pax River. We got in and it started like it was brand new. What a day it would be. We arrived at the spot where Floyd thought we should stop and began our hike to the lake he saw. Walking on the ground was like walking on sponges. The terrain was a little rolling but not steep. The grass was matted down and the trees were scrubby pine, not too high. The highest was probably about 6-7 feet in height and spread out. We walked about ½ hour when Floyd said the lake was just ahead. Sure enough, there it was. Not too big, about 2-3 acres in size. Those little pine trees seemed to line the lake shore with little interruption all around the lake. The sun was shining brightly and there was nary a cloud in the sky. The temperature was about 75 degrees. What a pretty picture it was. But as soon as we arrived at the lake the black flies started to gather around. We all sprayed ourselves from top to bottom. We really smelled of bug spray. It seemed to do the trick at that point.

We found a spot next to the shore where Jo could set up her fire and get ready to cook. Floyd and I tested the water. It was not cold. I was sure we wouldn't freeze or get cold wading out into the lake in our skivvies. We started the fire for Jo and she set herself up to cook. "When are you guys going to start fishing?" she said. "Get going. I'm not going to watch you get undressed. I want to see you when you come out of the water and you are soaking wet. Then I'll be able to see what I want to," she said laughing.

We undressed down to or skivvies and went into the water carrying our fishing rods over our heads. As we went deeper into the water the temperature was a little cooler than we expected. But we got used to it quickly as the fish began to bite. As soon as the flies we used hit the water the fish bit. Bang. They were small ones, medium size ones, but no large ones to speak of. We found out quickly that apparently there were more fish than food to support them. But, the medium sized trout were the ones we threw or carried over to Jo. As she fried them all three of us ate them, bones and all. When the fish fried in the pan they would turn the prettiest color salmon and the bones would basically melt. If the fish had been larger we had to be careful of the bones. After about 30 minutes of fishing, Jo said, "Enough for now. Come on out. Get warmed up and finish what I have cooked." We did exactly as she asked us to do, as we were getting cold.

The black flies were attacking our ears and a little blood was running down. We wrapped a towel around our heads and another around our bodies. Jo was laughing saying we looked like a couple of Arabs. I'm sure had we taken pictures of ourselves we would have had many laughs.

"How are the fish? Was this worthwhile? Do we want to fish some more and eat more fish?" Jo was full of questions. I can't blame her as we were fishing and eating and not saying much. We both answered positively in all cases. We asked her if she wanted to join us in the water and start fishing. She told us we were crazy and that if she went in it would be without clothes. Both Floyd and I agreed that would be ok with us. She almost threw the frying pan at us.

After eating more fish than we should have Floyd and I helped Jo clean up our mess, put out the fire and pack up to get ready to leave. Sitting by the fire had dried out our skivvies. Jo had brought extra towels for Floyd and me. What a great gal Jo Ivy was. She not only took care of Floyd, but also me. How lucky I was to have friends like this. We trekked back to the car and headed to Floyd and Jo's trailer. Jo kissed me goodbye, told me to be safe and Floyd and I headed to the base. He had to work that night, and I had to fly. It was the end of a perfect day fishing and enjoying each other's company.

Chapter 16

A Scary Night

I got back to the barracks to a "Where the hell have you been all day," from the boys. I explained where I had been and they asked where their fish was. No answer from me. I took a shower and got dressed for the mission. We all went down the hill to catch the eighteen wheeler. It was our transportation to the hangar for the mission briefing. There was nothing out of the normal given to us during the pre-brief other than the stormy weather we would experience out over the Atlantic. Because of the weather, communications may be difficult. We thanked the briefer and went down to our aircraft.

The pre-flight of the airplane was completed by Randal, Andy and Ensign Stahl. We all climbed the ladder and went aboard. It would be a normal flight. We had nothing to worry about. We had all been through stormy weather before and expected no real issues. Mr. Book taxied our plane out to the runway, was given clearance and made a normal take-off at 2000 hours Greenwich Mean Time. All of our flights were tracked on Greenwich Mean Time. Why Greenwich Mean Time? Greenwich Mean Time provides a common time for all Navy operations world wide. Mr. Nafis was navigating the first 7 hours and I was the radioman. It was getting bumpy as we left Argentia and the crew settled into a normal operation. Lt. Plover was running the CIC crew. Burgois, Celso, Harry, Frank and Larry were on duty, Bookie and LCDR Fox at the controls. Following take-off Bookie moved to the co-pilot's seat, Ensign Stahl slipped into the pilot's seat, LDCR Fox went to sleep and John was the flight engineer. The rest of the crew was settling in for a couple of hours' sleep.

Once we left the Newfoundland coast the early evening turned dark as clouds covered what was left of the sun. The air became choppier and I tightened my seat belt. As we approached the first check point Alpha, the weather turned worse and we began to experience rain and lightning.

There were three check points located across the Atlantic Ocean: Alpha, Bravo, and Charlie. The checkpoints were actually Navy destroyers deployed 300-400 miles apart down the barrier that were used for reporting bogies, getting radar fixes for navigation, and reporting aircraft positions. The ship's positions were basically fixed, but they actually sailed around in circles about 10 miles in diameter.

The plane started bumping harder. Larry from the CIC group came forward to me and asked, "Bruce, do you have communications with NWP7?" NWP7 was the Low frequency point of contact for Morse code transmission from the aircraft.

"Yes, I do," I replied. "Why? Don't you have voice communications with the ship at check point Alpha?"

"No, we don't," Larry responded. "During the last communication we had with them, they indicated that the weather was heavy and they lost some of their communication antennas and their radar was malfunctioning. They also told us that Checkpoint Bravo was out of service. We have a number of messages for you to send to NWP7."

He handed me 4 Zulu messages. Zulu messages were the highest priority of all messages. These were bogie reports. I sent them out immediately.

"Mr. Nafis, Larry from CIC advised me that Check point Alpha and Bravo were out of service due to storm damage." "Thanks Bruce," he replied. "I was able to get a position fix from Alpha 30 minutes ago". He continued, "Shit, no wonder I can't reach them any longer or get another radar position fix from them. I will have to dead reckon based on my last position fix 30 minutes ago."

The weather had become progressively worse. The airplane was bumping like a bucking bronco and about that time LCDR Fox called on the PA system and advised us to strap ourselves in as the weather was deteriorating quickly. He indicated that he had tried several different altitudes within the given range allowed and it was just as rough at these altitudes as it was at our normal altitude. He was awoken earlier by Bookie as the weather worsened. We would have to gut it out. He expected that this would last until 0100 Greenwich Mean Time. That was at least 1 and ½ hours to go. I looked out at the wing. LCDR Fox had turned on the lights that illuminated each wing. The rain was coming down in sheets. St. Elmo's fire was dancing on the leading and the trailing edges of the wings as well as the engine nacelles. This was the first time I had seen this phenomenon. St. Elmo's fire is a condition caused by the friction of the rain beating on the wing flying through it at air speed. The wing tips were flapping with each bounce up and down. From my position it looked as if they were moving 3 feet each way. The airplane was taking a beating. There was no voice communications with the ships down below. I was in touch with NWP7. It wasn't clear. I would hear static every time there was lightning or get a signal interruption, but the low frequency equipment was functioning and I could communicate.

I looked at my typewriter and the lines were wavy. The typewriter had a floating head on it and it went up and down as the airplane went up and down. My typing was wavy. The pre-briefer was right. We were encountering weather over the Atlantic. It was now approaching 2400 hours. We have about another hour to an hour and one half of rough weather to look forward to. Sure is fun. About this time I heard on the UHF Guard frequency 43 megacycles, "Unidentified aircraft identify your self. This is Navy 567." The Guard frequency is a universal channel on all UHF communication equipment. It is monitored continuously and is used to contact aircraft during emergency situations.

When I heard the call, I headed to the CIC Group to find out who was in trouble. I saw Mr. Plover, the CIC Officer digging in his briefcase, and Burgois looking dumbfounded. "Don, what is going on?" I asked.

"Bruce, we saw two aircraft on the radar come up from the south and position themselves off of each of our wing tips and then we hear over the guard frequency unidentified aircraft identify your self, this is Navy 567."

"What's going on?" I asked.

"Mr. Plover is looking for the Identification Friend or Foe code book to relay today's code. Once he does, and responds, it will be ok," Don tells me.

Mr. Plover relays the code.

"Unidentified aircraft, you have 60 seconds to identify yourself or we will shoot you down," comes across the Guard frequency again.

Mr. Plover looks at the time and turns white. "It's a new day," he exclaims. "Where's the new book?" Paper flies from his briefcase, and he finally finds the new book. He is racing through the pages to find the new code. He finds what he is looking for and says. "This is navy 141325 the code is—"

"Thank you Navy 141325. This is Navy 567. Good night."

Don and I watch the two aircraft on the radar break to the starboard and fly away. My body shivers.

Everyone lets out a sigh of relief. Mr. Plover looks as if the world has lifted from his shoulders as he slumps in his seat.

Larry says "We have almost been shot down. Someone reported us as a bogey. Where the hell are we?" He heads for the navigator.

"Mr. Nafis, we were almost shot down. Where are we?" Larry asks.

Just after he asked the question, LCDR Fox arrives at the navigator station, "Nafis, what the hell is going on? I have been monitoring the guard frequency. Where are we and what have you been doing? We apparently were reported as a bogey by one of our own airplanes".

It went downhill from that point. I never heard anyone be chewed out with expletives like Mr. Nafis was that night. I think if we would have been on a ship the LCDR would have physically thrown Mr. Nafis overboard or had him keel hauled. I'm sure this incident may have ended his career in the Navy. Apparently Mr. Nafis had been dead reckoning and forgot the wind or the weather. We were off course by over 100 miles and well within the bogey latitude and longitude necessary to be reported by one of our own.

During the excitement we did forget the weather. The plane was still moving pretty badly after the incident. We strapped in again and went back to business after we returned to course. We finally received a radar fix from one of our own aircraft. After another hour the weather began to clear and the aircraft settled down along with the remainder of the crew. Mr. Nafis was relieved by Mr. Stahl and we were able to return to the course we should have been flying on. We finally completed our mission safely that night no worse for the wear. Following our landing, we didn't see Mr. Nafis again. We missed Mr. Nafis as he was a sailors' officer. But, he wasn't a navigator. We all were happy to be back at Argentia safe and sound. It had been a scary night.

Chapter 17

Easter 1959

Bang, bang, bang!!! The watch came into the room to wake us up. We had asked to be awakened at 0100 that morning. "It is time to rise and shine. Happy Easter, gentlemen," he announced. "It's time to fly."

There were about 5 groans and some nasty words that sent the watch away. We all knew we had to fly that morning. We had the daily 0400 flight.

"What's the weather like?" Celso asked.

The watch responded, "It is a bit foggy out this morning, but nothing that you guys can't handle."

Harry rolled over as he did every day and picked up his pack of cigarettes from the top of the locker next to his bunk, took one out and lit it up let out a large puff of smoke.

"Harry, you're going to die one of these days from those lousy cigarettes," said Celso. Celso was the only one of the crew that didn't smoke.

"Knock it off, Celso," expressed Harry as he climbed out of the bunk. "I'll quit one of these days when I'm damn well ready."

Harry was always a grump in the mornings and Celso was always on his case.

Teenbeat came bouncing through the door singing his favorite song, Fats Domino's "Blue Monday." "Hey, guys, another Newfoundland beautiful day to fly," he noted loudly, to make sure all in the room were awake.

"Hey, guys, not so loud, it's to early in the morning. I'm still in the middle of a dream about my girlfriend," Dave said.

"Dave, take off you girlfriend's panties and get dressed," Jack ordered.

Jack looked like he was still hung over from his previous night's party at the petty officers club. Aubrey rolled over and fell to the floor. He slept in the lower bunk and was suffering from too much beer the night before. We were all up at about 0115 and starting to move around. There was a lot of grumping by all of the crew as it was a short night as always for a 0400 takeoff. We had to get dressed, get to early chow which would be waiting for us in enlisted men's chow hall at 0145 and board the eighteen wheeler at 0210 for the trip to the hangar. Flight briefing began on time at 0245, preflight the airplane at 0315, and ready to taxi at 0350. We had a tight schedule to be sure. No time for lollygagging around.

When we went outside and headed down the hill to board the eighteen wheeler, Frank exclaimed, "Oh my God, look at the fog. I can hardly see the truck. Is it down there? It is supposed to be there."

Don told Frank, "Come on Frankie boy, I'll hold your hand and lead you down the hill. Watch your step, little boy. Mommy will take care of you."

"Wow, thickest I've ever seen since I've been here," said Aubrey.

"You are still drunk from last night, Aubrey. Wake up and see the black night," Larry noted.

Down the hill we went moving slowly to make sure we didn't fall and roll down.

The truck was there. Its lights were trying to penetrate the thickest fog we had ever seen. "Do you think well fly tonight?" Celso asked.

"I don't know. We have flown in some pretty lousy weather before. We'll have to wait and see," I replied.

"At least it isn't snowing," Jack said laughing out loud.

As we got on the truck the driver told us he had a difficult time finding his way to the barracks in this thick mess.

Aubrey sarcastically told the driver, "I'll drive in this stuff drunk if that's what you want."

The driver ignored the comment. Every one booed Aubrey's words. The driver put the truck in gear and began to creep to the hangar. It seemed a long time for us to reach it. Normally it was 5 minutes. This morning the ride took 25 minutes!

When we reached the hangar we could hardly see the lights that illuminate the entire building. We exited the truck and went inside to get to the flight briefing. We were late due to the longer trip to the hangar. When I got there LCDR Fox wasn't there yet. The flight briefer was waiting for him to arrive.

Mr. Book asked us, "Where have you guys been? You're late."

We answered in unison, "The fog is so thick you could cut it with a knife. The truck took 25 minutes to get here, sir."

Bookie said, "Where I live up on the hill it was as clear as a night could be, but when I came down the hill, I had to open my car window and stick my head out the window to see two feet in front of the car. I bet LCDR Fox is having the same problem."

Sure enough, he was late. He was an anal person and his being late didn't make him very jovial this early morning.

When LCDR Fox opened the door to the briefing room, everyone stood up, he said, "As you were, let's get started as we will be late getting off the ground if we don't get moving. What a lousy day."

The briefer began the briefing with the weather. "The weather is clear over the Atlantic and over Newfoundland, Still some icebergs coming down. All picket ships are on station and running at 100%."

We all had quizzical looks on our faces when he mentioned the weather. But then the briefer covered the weather at Argentia.

"We are below minimums this morning, Gentlemen," he began. Visibility is 100 yards and ceiling is 100 feet at best. Wind is east at 3 knots. We are recommending waiting until fog lifts to at least 300 feet and ¼ mile visibility. Once you reach 500 feet you will break out into a clear sky."

LCDR Fox thanked the briefer and asked, "Is that all regarding the weather?"

"Yes, sir," replied the briefer.

LCDR Fox looks at Mr. Book and says, "Bookie, have operations get us a follow me truck for us to follow out to the end of the runway. Once we get to the end of the runway, we'll make a decision as to whether or not we will go."

"Yes, sir," replies Bookie.

We all then headed down to the hangar where our plane awaited us. Bill Murphy, our second flight Engineer, the third pilot Ensign Stahl, and Randal, my second radioman, were finishing up the preflight of the A/C. Operations had the follow me truck stationed in front of the A/C at the hangar door.

Once on board LCDR Fox came on the intercom and let us all know what was happening. "We will follow the follow me truck out to the end of the runway as we could not get there ourselves. We will then start the engines and run them up to get ready to take off. I will then contact the tower and check the weather again. Once we power up we will take our position for take off. I will then let you all know what we will do."

I looked out my window which was located over the port wing. I couldn't see anything except one runway light straining to get its light through the fog. The vehicle towing us started the A/C moving. He was following the follow-me truck.

After about 15 minutes, I heard the engines start and begin their run up. Finally LCDR Fox came back on the intercom, "Well, gentleman, we here in the cockpit have talked with the tower and the fog is thicker than ever. We can see three runway lights and the paint stripe down the middle of the runway. The engines run up fine. Once we achieve 500 feet of altitude we will have clear sky. I have decided to go. Fasten your seat belts. Here we go."

The next thing we heard was the engines turning up to take off speed. LCDR Fox released the brakes and the plane began to roll. Once the A/C speed reached 110 knots LCDR Box rotates and we felt the plane liftoff. I was looking out my window as the plane rose and sure enough as I look at the Navigators altimeter reaching 500 feet I began to see stars shining in the night sky. We were on our way this Easter Sunday 1959 to protect the USA. I sent our time of take off to NWP7 and wished them a Happy Easter from 25 knothole. They in turn wished us a Happy Easter. I looked forward and saw our electrician, Jack Bannister, carrying what looked like a ham. "Jack, what are you doing?" I asked.

"This is part of our Easter lunch. It's a ham. The commissary sent along a salad, sweet potatoes, rice and beans, apple pie, and even ice cream. What a deal for us today. Just like at home. Those guys in the commissary really take care of us," he replied. About then the navigator, Mr. Nafis, announced that we were on station and starting our barrier. The barrier that day was expected to be a routine flight.

About 4 hours into our flight LCDR Fox came on the intercom and announced that a VW-15 Super Connie had crashed after an emergency landing that morning. "I don't have any more information on the crew status at this time. When I get more info I will let you all know."

Our flight that day was routine as it could be, 16 hours in duration. Knowing that a WV had crashed at Argentia worried all of us as we knew many guys from VW-15. Jack did a magnificent job on our Easter dinner. Baked ham, scalloped potatoes, green bean casserole, tossed salad, coffee, real milk and a beautiful cake his wife made for us for dessert. The cake was white with chocolate frosting and bunnies all over it. What a wonderful meal under the circumstances.

As we approached Argentia, LCDR Fox came on the intercom again, "I know that we all are interested in what happened to the aircraft that crashed. Following our landing I will taxi down the runway to the crash area and give us all a chance to look out the starboard windows to see the WV that crashed."

We began another GCA approach to land again. The pilots and GCA were practicing, something we did for every landing at Argentia. Following touchdown LCDR Fox taxied down the runway so that we could look out the starboard window over the wing. The engines were in idle mode as our plane stopped to enable everyone to look out the window over the wing. Sure enough, there the WV was upside down, lying on the height-finding radar dome. The entire fuselage was black from the fire. It looked like the entire fuselage had burnt. Our entire CIC crew came to the window to look. The LCDR waited for at least 10 minutes on the runway so that everyone had a chance to see the airplane.

"I wonder how many of the crew was hurt?" wondered Burgois.

"I'm sure from what I see most of them were injured," noted Celso.

"I wonder what crew it was." I asked "I have a buddy who flies as a radar tech for VW-15. He was the other Bruce as we called each other."

"How did it happen?" remarked Ensign Nafis.

We all had a lot of questions, but no answers. We would be busy once we got back to the hangar. LCDR Fox turned up the engines and we taxied to the hangar.

Once we got there we headed to the de-brief. The LCDR in charge of the de-briefing started with the crash information we were all looking for. "It was the 0800 flight Easter morning. They too had a fog problem as you did. They used a follow me truck to get to the end of the runway. They turned up the engines. Everything checked out as normal. They took off in the same visuals that we did. Once airborne and about 200 miles out on the barrier they lost power in the number 3 engine.

The engine was feathered and fuel was dumped and the plane was turned back to Argentia. They had a full GCA landing in heavy fog and low ceiling. The GCA folks said it was a clean approach. The pilot acknowledged sighting the runway, but apparently hit the end of the runway hard and lost control of the A/C. The aircraft went up and came down on the nose wheel that collapsed and the A/C went completely over the front end and came down hard on the height finding radar antenna dome. It then skidded down the runway over three hundred feet and stopped. The crew immediately started to abandon the A/C. The crew was able to scramble out of the A/C before the fire began and quickly spread to the entire plane.

The entire crew with the exception of one was able to get out of the plane safely with only a few bruises. There was one fatality. He was AT1 John Down. He was a radar tech on the crew. Apparently when the A/C flipped over his chair broke loose and he bumped his head on the height finding radar console and was knocked out. The crew in their haste to leave the plane did not notice Down being knocked out. By the time the crew mustered outside of the A/C and noticed that Down was not with them, the plane was engulfed in flames and no one could go back inside to find him."

The briefer continued, "The crew was extremely fortunate that only one was lost in this accident." He advised, "A thorough investigation will be held. More information will be available following the investigation."

We debriefed our flight and went home to eat, clean up, and thank the lord for our normal flight. I'm sure we would play pinochle all through the night. We had to fly again in 48 hours and do it all over again.

Chapter 18

The Wedding

It was summer 1959. The 25 knothole crew was flying the normal schedule. Fly a mission, have 24 hours off, fly a mission have 24 hours off, fly a mission have 72 hours off and start the rotation again. It seems to be a lot of flying and a lot of time off. Once in a while we would get to work in the office or shop. But that was only if you couldn't fill in for someone who was on leave and needed a substitute to fly for them. But, we got used to the routine. We were surprised by Kent Fairchild advising us that he was getting married in about two months and asked a number of us to participate in or attend his wedding. Kent had joined the crew early in 1959 when Teenbeat left the Navy to get discharged. Kent was a kid that had grown up in a farming family in South Dakota. He decided to join the Navy to get off the farm and see the world as most of us had. He was also dodging the draft. He had met his intended Miss Vina Vey one weekend he spent with some of the guys in St. Johns, Newfoundland. St. Johns was where the girls of Newfoundland went to meet guys and the Navy guys went to meet Newfoundland girls. That is women who were Newfoundlanders as well as US Military wives who were bored at Argentia, and needed more than what Argentia could provide them. But, that's another chapter. Miss Vey was from a little town located in northeast Newfoundland called Little Hearts Ease. Population was 200. She was visiting St, Johns to meet some new friends and find the excitement that the largest city in Newfoundland offered.

They met at the hospital for the mentally ill. Vina was seventeen and a volunteer at the hospital. She had a date with someone else that night but Kent was following in another car. When Vina saw Kent with another guy who was meeting another volunteer that evening she decided to go out with him instead of the other guy. They double dated with the other couple. There was an immediate attraction and Kent was smitten. Kent and Vina became a couple almost immediately. He courted her via the Newfie bullet. The bullet was a train that ran from Argentia to the main line at Whitbourne This train line rode to Clarenville where Vina was a nanny for her friend Josephine. She had enough volunteering at the mental hospital and took the nanny job. Kent made this trip a number of times before he bought a 1952 Plymouth before the wedding. The car enabled him to travel to St. Johns from Argentia when ever he had time off. With our flying schedule it was difficult. But, where there is a will they found the way. It was a 50 mile trip to St. Johns on dirt roads from

Argentia and another 40 miles of dirt from St. Johns to Little Hearts Ease. Newfoundland had very few paved roads. The roads that were paved were mostly in St. Johns and on the base at Argentia.

Kent related the romance details to us and we could hardly believe that he found such a neat gal. She was a wonderful woman from a tiny town in Newfoundland and they were going to get married. When he asked me and Dave Bloomburg to stand up for him, we were honored that Kent picked us. We jumped at the opportunity to participate in the wedding. Dave replaced Randal as radioman when Randal was transferred to another crew. What a break being able to get out into the population and meet and visit some people from this province of Canada. Most of us visited St. Johns once or twice if we were lucky to get a ride, but this would be different. We knew very little about the province or its people.

Once the date was set, July 18, 1959, those of us in the wedding had to find some proper clothes to wear. The guys in the crew who were going to attend had the same problem. We didn't have very many civilian clothes as we were basically at the base most of the time. Argentia was not located close to a large city and the local town didn't offer much for us to do. We spent a lot of time in dungarees. We scrounged clothes from our buddies, bought shirts and ties from the Post Exchange and had clothes sent from home. We were excited. We were going to a wedding, with real people and real girls.

The wedding was being held in Clarenville. It was located about 90 miles on those dirt roads from Argentia. We hoped we would get a little rain for our trip to Clarenville to hold down the dust on the road. But, it didn't rain and the roads were very dusty. Kent drove up to Clarenville the day before the wedding. Vina didn't think Kent was even coming. Clarenville's claim to fame was that it was the location of the cable head for the AT&T Company overseas cable and close to some fabulous moose hunting. We stayed at the Clarenville Hotel, a small hotel that was used as a hunting lodge. It was a bit rustic but had hot and cold running water and great food. The hotel regularly hosted hunters and fisherman from all over the world. Newfoundland moose hunting and salmon fishing were at the top of the world's favorite list for hunters and fishermen from around the world. The crew split up into groups of four and stayed four to a room. Workers at the hotel were familiar with folks from outside of Newfoundland. But I'm sure they were not ready for a group of horny sailors from Argentia. When we arrived we were ready for a beer or a cold drink. The dust permeated the cars we were riding in and we were dusty and very thirsty. But, Kent had reminded us that we were guests in a foreign land and to be on our best behavior. We really tried to be the gentleman we were brought up to be and not ugly Americans.

The afternoon after we arrived, Kent finally got there and started with a little pep talk to the wedding party and other crew members. "Guys, this afternoon we are going to meet Nina's family and the ladies that you are standing up with. Please, no snide remarks, comments, or actions. The family and girls are a little concerned about you all. They have never met a group of Americans before and are a little apprehensive. I'm sure they have heard many stories about American sailors, so be on your toes tonight. We will have dinner and then Bruce, Dave, and I will go to the church to practice for the wedding tomorrow morning. The rest of you guys will be on your own. Please don't tear the place up. There is a bar here at the hotel. They know you are coming and are looking forward to having us as guests. Enjoy yourselves, but I don't want to have to pay for a wrecked bar."

The remainder of the crew assured Kent that they would be on their best behavior.

Dave and I met the family at the restaurant. "Dad and mom, or I should say Mr. and Mrs. Vey, I'd like you to meet my best man, Dave Bloomburg. He is from St. Louis, Missouri."

Dave responded in kind, "Very nice to meet you."

Kent continued, "This is Bruce Jarvis, my usher. He is from Cleveland, Ohio."

I responded, "Very nice to meet you."

Vina then introduced Dave and me to the girls we would be standing up with. "Dave and Bruce, this is Meana and Marne."

Dave and I looked at the girls and said, "Nice to meet you," with approving eyes. I was thinking to my-self, "Wow, a redhead and a blonde." Meana was a vivacious redhead and Marne was a beautiful blonde with piercing blue eyes. Dave would be standing up with the redhead and me the blonde. How lucky could we be? Kent took Vina's arm and led us all to our seats. We had a wonderful dinner at the hotel. Dinner included fresh salmon and moose meat from the past season. Fresh rolls, salad, and a delicious dessert completed the feast. To this day I'm not sure what it was, but it was fantastic.

Vina was all Kent told us about her. She was bubbly, vivacious, talkative and beautiful. Dave and I knew he was a lucky sailor. Her parents were very nice, though a bit reserved given it was the first time they were spending time with our group. The girls we were standing up with were very refined, but we could tell after meeting them, they loved to party. Following dinner Mr. and Mrs. Vey left to meet friends who were coming to the wedding. We thanked them for dinner and the wedding party left for the bar. We wanted a quick drink before we went to the church to practice for the wedding. We weren't the only ones at the bar. The other crew members were already there. Kent introduced the girls to the crew, we had a quick drink and left for practice.

As we arrived at the church and walked in, the Pastor was at the door and greeted us warmly. "How are you all? My name is Reverend Davis, I'm the pastor of the Clarenville United Church, where the wedding will be held tomorrow afternoon."

We all introduced ourselves. "I'm Bruce Jarvis, a friend of Kent's and a fellow crew member. I will be the usher in the wedding party." I offered.

"I'm David Bloomburg, a friend of Kent's and a fellow crew member. I will be Kent's best man."

The girls likewise introduced themselves to the Reverend. "I'm Mame Balus and am Nina's Maid of Honor".

"I'm Meana Strang and will be Nina's Attendant."

The Reverend took us inside the church. The small church was old and rustic. No doubt built by its members a number of years earlier. But in its own way reflective of its membership, plain, hard working and creative people who scratched their living from the land and sea. The church's windows were beautiful stained glass and were reflections of different scenes from the Bible. All were made by hand by the local members. The pews were hewn from local wood and the patina on them indicated to me that they are and have been well used over the years. Tomorrow the church would be decorated in all its finery. Right after we entered the church Nina's mom and dad came in behind us with some of their friends. Kent re-introduced us to her parents and to their friends. We began practice as soon as everyone was settled.

The Reverend began by telling us what the ceremony was going to be and led us through the procedure we were to follow. After he led us through the first time he told us that we had to go through it ourselves. The organist played the songs and we messed up the ceremony. So we had to do it again. I tripped and fell down. As I was falling I grabbed on to Meana to hold me up and down we went to the floor. As she went down her skirt went up and exposed a great set of legs and beautiful pink panties. She adjusted her skirt and looked at me. She seemed a little bit embarrassed. I looked at her and we both started laughing out loud. Well, that broke the ice. Everyone who was in the church laughed out loud. We practiced until we got it right, which took about an hour. By that time we were all ready for a drink and Dave and I were ready to talk to the girls and get to know them better.

The only bar in town was at the hotel. The bar looked like a hunting lodge and smelled like what is was. A moose head was mounted on one wall, a mess of large salmon mounted on another and many different beer and whiskey signs scattered and mounted around the room. There were two well used pool tables towards the back of the room. The bar was about 30 feet long with high stools and located in one corner was a juke box with 40's and some 50' songs on it. There was a small dance floor located between the bar and pool table with a number of small tables scattered around the room. It was very warm and comfortable.

About that time a number of girls from town came into the bar, along with a number of 25 knothole crew members. Where they met, to this day I still have no idea. My guess is that it had to be at the hotel. One thing for sure they were in a party mood. We also found out after introductions, that the women would be attending the wedding reception. They were all Vina's friends. It looked as if we were off to a great start. It was about 2030 when the party started. The girls all drank Canadian Club whisky and the guys did the same with the exception of the beer drinkers. They drank Molson's beer and ale. The level of conversation increased and the juke box began to play. The juke box played Big Band music to boogie to and rock and roll ballads to slow dance to.

The night roared on. The music got slower and the people a bit drunk. It was obvious that there were a number of male and female attractions happening. We all played a continuous 9 ball pool game. Everyone at the party was involved in the game. The bartender kept the drinks and the juke box busy for us. We told him to keep a tab open through the night. All the crew would split the bill at the end of the evening. By 2300 when the last call was made there was a lot of kissing and close dancing going on. The problem we were going to have was, where could they find a place to go with the girl they were with if a physical attraction were to develop? Egads, we never thought of that. We said good night to the girls and all of us headed to the hotel. We had an exciting day to look forward to in the morning.

It was tough getting up in the morning, but with the wedding starting at 0900 sharp the crew had to be in church and those of us in the wedding party had to be ready to go a he hotel at 0830 hours. Dave, Kent, and I were on time. We each had a shot of Canadian Club and we made sure Kent was fortified and had at least two shots. We left for the church. "Kent, are you sure you want to do this?" asked Dave.

"We can get to the car and take off if you want," I told Kent.

"Guys, I' m ready to do this. Ever since I met this gal I've been ready," he responded. "She meets all my criteria."

"Are you sure she isn't marrying you just to get out of Newfoundland and become an American citizen?" asked Dave. I thought Kent was going to belt him.

"He is just doing his job as best man," I told Kent.

"Hey, guys, I know you are looking out for me, but I am ready to marry this woman for better for worse and all that stuff. Let's get to the church. We have to go in the back door and get to the front of the church before Vina and the girls come down the aisle."

We opened the church door and walked in. The Reverend met us in the rectory and asked, "Are you ready to go?"

We all responded at once, "Yes, Reverend."

I snuck a look out the rectory door and said to Dave and Kent, "Look at the Church. Someone spent a lot of time decorating the church last night while we were partying." The church looked beautifully decorated with white and blue ribbons up and down the aisle and beautiful flowers placed on the altar. The sun was shining through the stained glass windows and the overall scene was just gorgeous. What a place and day for a wedding.

I went to the back of the church and began ushering folks to their places. About 15 minutes later the bridal party arrived. Wow! Vina and the girls were just beautiful, Vina wore a gown of white satin with a bodice embroidered with cup sequins and simulated pearls, fashioned with tapered sleeves. The satin skirt had two over skirts of nylon net. Her veil of nylon net with embroidered design was held by halo of nylon tulle with rayon plush and flower trim. She carried a beautiful bouquet of pink and white roses with lily of valley sprigs and fern with a large white bow and streamers. The girls wore gowns of powder blue taffeta and boleros of nylon net. Their skirts were fashioned with several layers of nylon net. They wore a matching halo and carried bouquets of red and white carnations and fern. Both girls looked stunning to say the least.

I knew Kent would be very proud when he saw Vina start down the aisle from the back of the church. As soon as I had everyone seated I moved to the front of the church behind Dave and Kent. We waited to begin. Most of the girls from last night's party were there. I'm sure they had headaches as we did. The church door opened and to the strains of Lohengrin's Bridal Chours, the procession began with Meana leading, followed by Mame, and then Nina being escorted by her Dad. As they reached the front of the Church her Dad kissed Vina and handed her over to Kent. The Reverend said the words and while Kent and Vina signed the roster, the soloist sang "The Lord is my Sheppard." The Reverend then had the couple kiss, turn around and he introduced Mr. and Mrs. Kent Fairfield to the world. The Reverend proudly said, "Ladies and Gentleman, I proudly introduce Mr. and Mrs. Kent Fairfield."

Everyone in the church clapped and cheered. We, Dave, Meana, Mame, and I followed Kent and Vina out of the church. We all waited at the front of the church for the folks in the church to file past us and congratulate the Bride and Groom. As we left the church the rice flew. It was an amazing scene. Everyone was smiling and cheering the Bride and Groom. It was a happening in Clarenville, Newfoundland that day.

After we left the church Dave and I kissed Vina with big juicy kisses and shook Kent's hand congratulating them both. "We are now going to the Reverend's house for some refreshments and a talk to us by the Reverend," said Kent.

Vina popped in and told us, "This is a Newfoundland tradition. The Reverend speaks to the wedding party before the reception that evening."

The Reverend's wife served champagne and sweets to us all and made small talk with the wedding party, while we ate them. Being from the United States all three of us were somewhat shocked to see that only the wedding party was there and not the rest of the guests for what turned out to be a qwazi breakfast, Cakes and tea. No wine or whiskey. The small talk was full of congratulations and where we were all from and how and why we joined the Navy. The Reverend's wife was very nice and wanted to make sure all of us were happy and comfortable.

The Reverend then began his little talk. He talked about Vina, where she was from, where she grew up, her education, her parents and some of her family history. It was very interesting. He then asked us about our selves. We each told about ourselves. Kent explained that he was a farm boy from South Dakota who wanted to see the world instead spending the rest of his life being a farmer. Dave started with the fact that he came from a poor family and wanted to improve his lot in life. He was from St. Louis, Missouri, a city located on the Mississippi. He joined the Navy to get a job. I explained that I was from a small town called Garfield Heights, Ohio which was located outside of Cleveland, Ohio. I then tried to explain where Ohio was located and confused every one. We all laughed about that

"I graduated from Garfield Heights High School in June of 1956. I was planning to attend college that fall, but my Dad couldn't afford to send me, so without any money or education I decided to join the Navy to get an education and see the world. So here I am. I am the radio man on the crew."

Following our histories, the Reverend began, United States service men have been stationed here in Newfoundland for over 15 years. The President of the United States, Franklin Roosevelt, met with British Prime Minister Winston Churchill in Placentia Bay, which is adjacent to Argentia, to discuss War Strategy. From the earliest date United States service men were stationed here in Newfoundland, Newfoundland women took a shine to them. I'm sure you all have noticed that Newfoundland men don't take kindly to US servicemen. One of the reasons is that you all have more money to spend on our women than our men do. The women made their preference obvious, since the United States service men came to Newfoundland they have taken more than 37,000 of our women home with them. Kent will do the same with Vina when he leaves the base for a new duty station. So you can see why there is a little resentment of the US serviceman by our men."

It was an interesting informative discussion. The Reverend suggested that we go back to the lodge and get some rest before tonight's reception. We all agreed and thanked the Reverend and his wife for their hospitality.

When we reached the lodge we stopped at the bar to get some hair of the dog and ran into the crew who had been drinking beer to help sober up from the previous evening. They had breakfast and were feeling pretty good. The reception would not get started until 1730. We had a few hours to spend, so we started a pool tournament to pass the time. The crew was wondering if the gals we met the night before would be attending the reception. Dave didn't know and neither did I. "If they don't," I said, "I'm sure there will be more."

Kelly one of our radar techs, commented, "This place is so small; there can't be many more girls around. Hopefully they will all be at the reception. If not we'll just dance with the old ladies."

The pool game lasted the remainder of the day into the afternoon. We drank beer and relaxed. We met Kent at 1700 coming into the lodge.

"Where have you been?" Dave asked.

"I've been with Vina's family and friends drinking Champaign, celebrating, and taking pictures. How much Canadian Club do we have?" asked Kent.

"Let's see," I said. "We brought two cases of 40 ounce bottles. We have 24 bottles. Will that be enough? If not, does the lodge have any?"

"Damn if I know," Kent retorted. "Let's get dressed and head over to the Canadian Legion Hall. Remember, crew, we are visitors here. Be good sailors."

"Right," we all answered in unison.

We all walked over to the hall, opened the door and walked in. We were the first ones there other than the bartender and the band that was setting up. Kent went over and talked to the bartender. We took the CC and gave it to the bartender. He commented, "That is a lot of booze, I hope it will last."

Dave and I looked at each other and said, "I hope it will last?"

The bartender said, "These folks are big drinkers, but I have a few more bottles here in the bar. We should be OK. By the way who will pay the additional cost if there is any?"

Kent told the bartender, "Vina's Father will pay any tab that is left over."

The bartender said, "Ok, have a great time, guys, just don't break anything or I'll have to call the Mounties."

"No problem," Kent said, "They won't."

Vina, her family, Marne and Meana came into the hall along with all the girls we met the night before. Guests continued to come in until about 1830. The crew was back meeting the girls and Kent, Dave, and I found Vina, Marne, and Meana to find out what events were going to happen that evening.

Vina explained, "There will be a bride and groom dance, a family dance, garter throw, a bouquet throw, a cake cutting, and you Dave and I will participate."

Dave and I agreed, "Yes Ma'm."

She was the boss. The music started and off we went. Meana introduced her boyfriend and Mame introduced her husband. Both of them seemed like nice fellas and were built like tanks.

Mame took me aside and told me her husband drank a lot, but was harmless when she was around. She explained, "Meana's boyfriend was very jealous and also liked to drink but he is a light weight and would pass out about 900pm."

I laughed about it. She continued, "Don't look for the fancy pink panties you saw when you pulled her down in the church. She decided to not put any panties on tonight to make things easier on who ever she fancies tonight."

"Wow!" I replied. How about you? I said, "Do you have on panties?"

She replied, "You'll have to find out yourself, won't you?"

The reception began and the band began to play. It will be a fun night. The bar was open and the line at the bar was moving quickly. Kent and Vina were seeing all the attendees and Vina was being kissed by all. The crew made sure they got theirs. Everyone was drinking Canadian Club. By 900pm Meana's boyfriend was out like a light. He had been drinking shots with the crew. Mame's husband was holding his own. We danced with everyone, even Vina's mother and grandmother. All the events scheduled to happen came off like magic. During the bridal party dance we all switched off. Everyone danced with everyone.

While dancing with Mame, she pressed her body against mine so tight you couldn't get a piece of paper between us and she whispered in my ear. "I want you, but I can't figure out when and how. Think about it."

My Johnson responded very quickly. I found it difficult to let her go when the dance was over as my pants were bulging. I put my hands in my pockets and kind of leaned over to hide the bulge and walked off the floor to sit down and contemplate the next move.

I looked around and there was Kelly dancing with Meana squirming himself. Wow! We were having a night. Everyone was having a great night. It was a kissing night. Kent and Vina were having a big time dancing with everyone and drinking shots and glasses of CC with whoever offered. The band wasn't bad and seemed to get better as the night wore on. The crew was having a ball. The girls we met the night before danced with everyone. They all seemed to be scoring themselves. We had a problem. It was the where and when issue. We might have to wait until a St. Johns visit could be arranged. All of the special events Vina told us were going to happen came off just as planned. It was a beautiful night for a great couple.

As the party went on, I danced with Marne again. I was a little bit afraid of what her husband might do. "Marne what about your husband? He must see we are dancing close and rubbing each other in public."

"He doesn't dance or even see us out here. He is drinking with his buddies and telling hunting stories," she replied.

She did it again; she pressed her body against mine and rubbed it against me. This time Johnson was already standing at attention. She moved it between her legs and brought her body as close at it can get on the dance floor. I asked her, "Can you and I meet in St Johns."

"No," she couldn't get away, maybe in Argentia". That was it and that dance was over. I had that bulge issue again but I was tipsy enough not to care. Kelly and Meana were nowhere in sight. Her boyfriend was passed out in a chair in a corner of the hall. It was getting late and Kent and Vina were getting ready to leave.

We all yelled, "Good by," and Kent kind of staggered out with Vina. Vina was directing him out the door. They were headed to St. Johns for their honeymoon.

Dave and I followed them to the Plymouth to make sure they would get on their way safely. We kissed Nina again, shook Kent's hand and watched them leave up the road. What we didn't know was that the road to St. Johns out of

Clarenville was very curvy with a number of steep hills. It turned out as Kent reached the top of one of the hills he leaned over to kiss Vina at 30 mph. In the middle of the clinch, the road curved and the car went off the road and down the bank. The car came to rest upside down with the roof and windshield laying on a large rock.

Kent and Vina crawled out the side window and left the car overnight. No one was hurt. They were both very loose. The Canadian Club did it. Where they ended up that night, only they know. The next morning a wrecker got the car upright and towed to Clarenville. Kent managed to pound out the roof, pieced the windshield together and drove the car to St. Johns. They had a great day, a wonderful wedding, a great party and an interesting, eventful trip to St. Johns.

What else could our crew want but to spend a weekend like the one we just had? To this day we don't know where Kent and Vina spent that first night. Kent says at the lodge. Vina won't say. The crew checked out of the lodge, jumped back in the car and headed back to Argentia on those dusty roads. We had to fly the next morning. On the way home the war stories began. Kelly did make it with Meana. It took place in her car. He said he was surprised that she didn't have panties on. He hoped to see her again in St. Johns.

The other guys enjoyed themselves, but didn't have any physical exchanges. They all made future plans with the ladies they met. We all managed to stagger back to the lodge. We all did get drunk and forgot how we got back to the lodge. A good time was had by all. We all agreed that the folks from Newfoundland sure knew how to have a party and are wonderful people. We didn't embarrass Kent and Nina. After all, we were United States sailors' and gentlemen.

Appendix 1

The Plane

"The Queen of the Skies" is what Claude G. Luisada called the Lockheed Constellation in his book of the same name. Mr. Luisada takes one from the initial design of the Lockheed Constellation through the aircraft's life history and its usages. He completely details the evolution of its design and changes. This is the aircraft that was modified by Lockheed Corporation to meet the Navy and Air Force requirements to fly the barriers in defense of the United States of America from 1954-1967.

The Air Force was the first military service whose role in this mission was clearly defined. It was manning the two barriers, which were closer to the shore. The Navy was to staff the two barriers further off-shore, but their mission was spelled out after the Air Force's, even though the Navy pioneered the type of aircraft, tested it, helped design the production aircraft and had placed the first orders for it. Lockheed suggested that the order for Super Constellation C121C transports be changed to one for RC121-C AEW&C Aircraft. Lockheed gave the plane the name "Warning Star," which was used for all of the airplanes as well as the general program.

The aircraft the Navy was talking to Lockheed about was known initially as the PO-2W. This was changed to the designation WV-2. The WV-2 was a direct outgrowth of the PO-1W prototype airplanes which the Navy developed with Lockheed only a couple of years earlier. The Navy had been considering ordering the PO1W airplane into production as the two prototypes had been highly successful. But, another Lockheed representative came on the scene and suggested that a larger antenna be placed on the aircraft such as the 17.5 foot antenna the Navy developed for its blimp program to replace the originally designed 6 foot antenna for the prototype. He recommended that the antenna be placed on the bottom of the aircraft. This resolved a lot of problems the engineers had been having. Thus it was suggested to the Navy to purchase a new radar picket aircraft based on the newly designed Super Constellation and mount the larger antenna.

The aircraft design with this radome modification and new 3350 Turbo-compound engines engineered to lift much greater weights gave the Navy a design that would have more internal space for electronics and crew and a greater fuel load for a much increased barrier time. So it was in the mid 50s that the Navy began contractual talks with Lockheed to purchase quantities of the new radar picket airplane.

Because the decisions as to the actual responsibilities for the AEW operation came over a period of time, the aircraft acquired by the Navy and Air Force were placed on order at various dates. For this reason the aircraft were delivered over an extended period of time and the total AEW concept was implemented over a three year period. The initial order for Navy Aircraft was to carry out fleet defense operation and had nothing to do with the continental U.S. air defense mission. The same seems to be true for the second and third orders for the Navy. It is important to understand that the Navy role in AEW was not formalized until late 1954. This decision resulted in large Navy orders of WV-2's in fiscal years 1955 and 1956. From October 1953 through September 1958 the Navy purchased 142 WV-2s. The Navy ordered an additional 8 WV-3s. These aircraft were fully operational AEW aircraft but, had additional equipment for weather reconnaissance, especially for hurricane tracking and analysis. From October 1953 to October 1956 the Air Force ordered 82 RC121C & RC121D aircraft.

The WV-2/RC121D aircraft bears some careful scrutiny as it was a truly unique airplane. The basic airplane was identical in its dimensions to all other Super Constellations, except the last model. It had a wing span of 123 feet, a fuselage length of 116 feet, 2 inches and an overall height of 24 feet 8 inches at the top of the tail fins. However, the external appearance was very different from other Super Constellations. The aircraft was powered by 4 Curtis Wright Turbo Compound Engines. Above the fuselage directly over the wing jutted a plastic radome not unlike a shark's fin in appearance. This structure housed the APS-45 height finding radar antenna and measured eight feet high. It had a tear dropped cross-section to reduce drag. Directly beneath the wing was attached a bowl shaped radome. It housed the antenna for the APS20B long range radar. It measured some 19 feet by 29 feet by 4 feet with a mere 14 inches of ground clearance. In addition to the radomes, the aircraft had the first appearance of wing tip gas tanks. The aircraft had a maximum overload take-off weight of 143,000 pounds. Its 10 fuel tanks including the wingtip tanks carried a grand total of 8750 gallons of fuel. With a full fuel load the WV Aircraft could fly for 16-20 hours.

During the initial period of operations, a number of problems arose under the stress of daily operations. The Turbo-Compound engines were shown to be strong and reliable power plants provided they were operated and maintained according to the manufacturer's directions. If they weren't, problems multiplied quickly and time between overhauls was reduced accordingly. Pilots and flight engineers who had been dealing with less powerful engines just couldn't bang the throttles open or operate at maximum take power for longer periods of time than specified in flight manuals. Another issue was spark plugs. They were unreliable. In May and June 1956 the Navy experienced 2000 spark plug failures. Another difficulty was leaking oil tanks. The Warning Star did not have self sealing tanks. The Air Force had radar malfunction the first 6 months of 1957.

The problems encountered with, over time were corrected. The aircraft met the needs of the mission. The plane flew in all weather conditions, rain, sleet, snow, severe icing, heavy turbulence, hurricanes, lightening, Saint Elmo's fire, high and low temperatures, and came out on top. Of course there were engine failures, but the Aircraft could fly on three engines without difficulty. Barrier patrols flew for 6 years 7 days per week, 24 hours per day 365 days per year without let up. The reliability of the Warning Stars was nothing short of phenomenal.

Maintenance requirements were very clearly spelled out in the "Morning Star" Maintenance manuals. Lockheed noted very strongly that each aircraft had to have 100, 200, and 300 hour overhaul checkups by each squadron's maintenance personnel and a 400-hour complete overhaul by Lockheed Air service located at Idlewild airport on Long Island in New York and at Honolulu, Hawaii International for aircraft located in the Pacific. These included complete testing of all electronic equipment.

Appendix 2

The Weather and Barrier Squadrons

The Navy commissioned Airborne Early Warning Atlantic at Naval Air Station Patuxent, River Maryland on July 1, 1955 with the three member squadrons activated on August 1, September 1, and October 1. The Squadrons were VW-11, VW13, and VW-15. On May 1, 1956 the wing moved to Argentia, Newfoundland. On July 1, 1956 the Atlantic Barrier was initiated on a full time basis. While the Navy began its full-time operation, operational flights over the Atlantic, the Air Force began its portion over the Pacific. Each service then initiated its second phase on the opposite side of the North American continent. The Air Force began its Atlantic operation from Otis Air Force Base on Cape Cod. The Navy began its Pacific Barrier from Oahu, Hawaii with VW 12, VW-14, and VW-16. The Air Force began its Pacific barrier from McClellan AFB in California.

Manning the new squadrons by both the Navy and Air Force presented the services with a difficult task to say the least. Both services had a new mission, a new complex aircraft, new processes and few experienced people to start their barriers. Flight engineers had to be trained on new aircraft with new engines and complex procedures in a multi-engine environment. Pilots had to be certified in a new aircraft. Maintenance personnel and electronics personnel had to be trained on the maintenance of new equipment. Many new ACW rated personnel had to be trained to operate their critical function of identifying and reporting bogies while flying the Atlantic and Pacific barriers rather than operating out of towers.

Most of the crews and maintenance personnel were new to the Navy and their roles in flying the barriers. The recruiting, training and moving the right personnel to the right spots during a very short timeline, 1954-56, took thousands of existing Navy and Air Force personnel to man and plan the new squadrons' operations. The mission was accomplished but at times was very difficult. Once the initial planning was accomplished by the Air Force and Navy Staffs, the hard work began. It started with the administrative personnel, Recruit Commands, Training Commands, and the various Squadron Commands.

Finally, it was up to the Officers, Chief Petty Officers, Master Sergeants and the individuals of the Squadrons themselves to make it happen. Most of us were

18 to 23 years old, new Ensigns, 2nd Lieutenants and airmen, just out of boot camp, aviation training and the Service academies or Officer training schools. We were proud to be airdales and were told how important our mission was. We were told the critical nature of the mission and that we were expendable. Most of us didn't know what that meant, but it didn't take long to know that we would be replaced as soon as we were gone, disabled, or dead. The mission was that important. We were protecting our country from the Soviet Union, we all saluted and said "Aye, Aye, Sir," and went on.

The Airborne Early Warning Squadrons that flew EC121 and WV Lockheed Super Constellations were born 1955. They were initially developed to extend the Distant Early Warning Line (DEW) line from Canada to the east over the Atlantic Ocean and west over the Pacific. Although missions were added and rearranged over time, the Squadrons primary purpose was Airborne Early Warning. Every Squadron participated in special missions. All participated in air searches for military aircraft, civilian boats at sea, civilian aircraft, and various medical missions. Every Squadron received military awards for their accomplishments while doing their assignments. The following is a short history of each Air Early Warning Squadron established by the Navy. I'm sure members of each squadron have many memories and can provide a much more detailed history of their squadron. Hopefully, this information will be fully documented by these personnel so that this information will not be lost. Future generations will need to know what these organizations accomplished flying an aircraft that has gone down in history as one of the most accomplished. The Squadrons were the ones that flew Airborne Early Warning, Anti-submarine, and Weather Reconnaissance missions. They flew in the worst weather that Mother Earth could produce, survived, and completed their missions. This Aircraft is the Lockheed Super Constellation known as the Willy Victor (WV), EC 121, or Morning Star. It was one of, if not the, most reliable and rugged that the Navy and Air Force has ever flown.

VW-1—was established June 18, 1952 at Naval Air Station Barbers Point, Territory of Hawaii, as an outgrowth of VC-11's detachment which had recently arrived at Naval Air Station Barbers Point from NAAS Miramar, California. VW-1's first aircraft was the PB-1W. VW-1 received its first Lockheed Constellation in December 1952. This aircraft was initially designated PO-1W which was later changed to WV-1. It was the radar version of the civilian version of the Lockheed Constellation 749 or "baby connie." A permanent detachment of VW-1 was established in the Western Pacific and flew out of the Philippines, Okinawa, and Japan. It provided early warning cover for the seventh fleet. Another WV-1 and crew was attached to the Atomic Energy

Commission and provided support for A-Bomb testing in 1952. VW-1 also participated in the Korean War. VW-1 crews also flew missions over the Tachen Islands of Matsu and Quemoy in 1955. VW-1 also flew patrols over the Tiawan Straits during 1957.

VW-1 received its first WV-2 in April 1954 and transferred its last PB-1W in February 1955. In 1957 VW-1 moved its home port from Naval Air Station Barbers Point, Hawaii to Naval Air Station Agana, Guam. In July 1960 VW-1 absorbed many men and aircraft from VW-3. In July 1961 was given the additional task of weather reconnaissance. The reconnaissance territory began with the International dateline, ran west to the Malaysian Peninsula and from the Equator north. During 1961 VW-1 flew over 1000 hours tracking typhoons and storms. VW-1 became the "Weather Trackers". Weather flights usually lasted 12-16 hours. They included two storm penetrations, one at 1500 feet or below and one at the 700 millibar level which was determined during the first penetration. In addition the flight also determined the wind velocity and direction of the storm and made drops and observations. VW-1 super constellations were equipped with meteorological equipment in addition to the standard configuration. This additional equipment supported weather reconnaissance missions. During the later 1960s the VW-1 Constellations electronic equipment was upgraded to Doppler navigation systems and an improved radio altimeter. Also Aerographer stations were equipped with bubble window observation stations behind the CIC platforms.

During the Viet Nam War following the Gulf of Tonkin incident in August of 1964, additional requirements were placed on VW-1 to fly regular daily night-time early warning flights in support of combat operations in Southeast Asia. A permanent attachment was sent to the western Pacific to accomplish this mission. They flew out of Sangly Point or Cubi Point from 1964 to 1967. The barrier ran from 20 degree track on an East-West direction between Hainan Island and the Coast of Viet Nam. The flying time was usually 14-15 hours. Crews were rotated to and from Guam as weather reconnaissance flights continued to be flown. On December 18, 1967 VW-1 established a detachment at Chu Lai, RVN later moving to Da Nang RVN. This was done to spend more time on station for Airborne Early Warning coverage for the Seventh Fleet. In 1966 VW-1 celebrated 100,000 accident free flying hours. Between 1968 and 1970 VW-1 received an additional tasking. VW-1 sent a detachment to California for weather reconnaissance along the West coast of the Americas and to support NASA for Apollo space missions and NASA support in the Pacific. VW-1 was disestablished on July 1, 1971. VW-1 flew 160,000 Accident free hours during its tenure of 19 years.

VW-2—was established as VP-11 F on July 1936. It was re-established as VP-11 Oct 1, 1937, re-established VP-54 July 1, 1939, re-designated VP-51 July 1, 1941, re-designated VB-101 March 1, re-designated VBP-101 October 1, 1944, re-designated Aircraft Development Squadron 4VX-4 May15, 1946, re-designated Airborne Early Squadron (AEW) VW-2 June 18, 1952. VW-2 as an Airborne Early Warning squadron primary mission was to provide airborne Command and Control (CIC) services to second and sixth fleet and shore warning nets. VW-2 was home based at Naval Air Station Patuxent River, Maryland. VW-2 had planes located at Naval Air Station Patuxent River, Maryland, Keflavik, Iceland, Halfar, Malta, and Sigonella, Sicily. VW-2 was decommissioned July 1, 1961.

VW-3—On March 19, 1952 Airborne Early Warning Squadron Three (VW-3) was commissioned as Weather Squadron One (VJ-1) at Seattle, Washington. In July 1952, VJ-1 moved to Naval Air Station, Agana, Guam. The squadron was equipped with 6 P4Y-2 S aircraft. VJ-1's primary mission was to provide weather reconnaissance in the Pacific area for Fleet Weather Central in Guam. Following one and one half years of service the squadron designation was changed from VJ-1 to Airborne Early Warning Three. Following re-designation her aircraft were converted to P2V-5JF Neptune aircraft. VW-3's mission remained the same as VJ-1. In October 1955 VW-3 received the first of its WV-3 Weather equipped Radar Super Constellations. In late 1956 WV-3's primary mission changed from weather reconnaissance to airborne early warning for the Seventh Fleet. Weather reconnaissance became WV-3's second mission. In 1957 the last of VW-3's Neptune and WV3 aircraft were phased out and replaced with twelve WV2 aircraft. VW-3's Super Constellations also flew out of Okinawa, Japan and the Philippine Islands. Normal Operations included alternating five week shifts with VW-1 providing Airborne Early Warning support to the seventh Fleet. VW-3 regularly provided navigational assistance for jet and single engine aircraft in the Pacific area. Since moving to Guam VW-3 flew 41,500 hours. On June 30, 1960, VW-3 was decommissioned.

VW-4—In 1952 Weather Squadron VJ-2 was commissioned at NAS Miami to replace VP-23 and was still using PB4Y-2 Privateers. After moving to Jacksonville, VJ-2 "Hurricane Hunters" began taking delivery of P2V-3W "Neptunes" during the 1953 hurricane season. Following the 1953 hurricane season VJ-2 was decommissioned and Airborne Early Warning Squadron 4 (VW-4) was established. Initially VW-4 flew P2V-3W aircraft. In 1954, WV-1 aircraft were assigned to VW-4 to augment the Neptunes. In 1955 the WV-1 was replaced the WV-3 Super Constellation weather configured early warning aircraft and the P2V-3W were replaced by the jet modified P2V-5JF Neptunes.

The first hurricane eye is penetrated by Super Constellation radar. The hurricane was named IONE. On September 26, 1955 a P2V was lost penetrating Hurricane Janet near Swan Island. All hands were lost. In 1957 the Super Constellation is used for regular hurricane reconnaissance. In 1958 the P2V Neptune is phased out. In 1960 the VW-4 "Hurricane Hunters" moved from Jacksonville to U. S. Naval Station, Roosevelt Roads, Puerto Rico. In January 1965, VW-4 returned to Jacksonville and maintained a year around detachment at Puerto Rico which provided weather surveillance in the Caribbean and Atlantic on a year around basis. In 1971 VW-4 began taking delivery of WP-3A "Orions" to replace the tired old Connies. As the Orions were faster and had longer range than the Connies, The detachment at Roosevelt Roads was removed. VW-4 was disestablished in April 1975, having logged 80,000 accident free hours over 17 years. Over 13,000 hours were logged in actual hurricane reconnaissance.

VW-11—Airborne Air Early Squadron ELEVEN (VW-11) was commissioned August 1, 1955 at Naval Air Station Patuxent River (Pax River). Initial aircraft that were received were R7Vs. These were used for pilot training. CIC officers were sent to VW-2 to fly with their crews for training. The first WV-2 craft arrived in the middle of November 1955 and barrier training began. Short barriers were flown at the start (6 hours) and long barriers later (12-14Hours). By the middle of April 1956, VW-11 had 16 qualified crews and a full complement of WV-2s. An advance party of officers and enlisted men were sent to Argentia to get things ready for deployment. This would be the first time a squadron of this size would be deployed out side of the continental United States (135 Officers and 600 enlisted men). This was a move from scratch. The logistics were complex and difficult. VW-11 accomplished this mission on time for its first scheduled official Atlantic Barrier 1, July 1956. VW-11 returned to Patuxent River on October 6, 1956 following 2 months of developing a routine and 3 months of normalcy with crews flying approximately 30 hours per week. VW-11 almost immediately following its return to Patuxent River received orders to redeploy to Argentia. On November 5, 1956 in a matter of three to five hours, almost the entire squadron and its planes had departed for Argentia. Once back to Argentia the squadron prepared for an indefinite stay. Plans were set for a heavy operations schedule. On the evening of November 20, 1956 received orders to return to Patuxent River. As quickly as the Squadron left Pax River it returned. On July 1, 1957 VW-11 returned to Argentia. The new hangar was completed by their return. On this deployment VW-11 returned with its sister squadron VW-13. VW-11 had now grown to 140 officers and 810 enlisted men. Flight operations continued with both squadrons flying the Barrier until September of 1957 when VW-13 was de commissioned. VW-11 remained as the only Squadron flying the Barrier. On December 1,

1957 VW-11 returned to Pax River. In January 1958 orders were received to augment the Atlantic Barrier by VW-11 crews. VW-11 headquarters remained at Pax River and the main body of personnel also stayed home. The first crews left for Argentia on 14 January 1958. It was by coincidence that also on this date VW-11 lost its first Aircraft. R7V128437 crashed at Pax River during a routine training flight. All hands were lost.

On 29 April 1958 VW-11 received orders to change its home port from Pax River to Argentia Newfoundland effective 1 August 1958. Plans were made to move 700 dependants and the squadron which had grown to 170 officers and 1063 enlisted men. This was accomplished by 20 August 1958. The worst winter in 20 years hit Newfoundland that year. The Atlantic barrier was maintained throughout. On March 3, 1961 the 10,000th Atlantic Barrier was flown. On 1 August 1961 VW-11 flew the last Atlantic Barrier out of Argentia. VW-11 deployed its crews to Keflavik, Iceland to fly a new barrier in conjunction with the Icelandic defense. The new barrier was the Green-Iceland-Great Britain Barrier. This detachment was known as Detachment 13 and remained until VW-11 was decommissioned. On August 3, 1963 VW-11 received its first WV-2 modified with anti submarine warfare (ASW) equipment. The modified WV2 was the first of its kind within the Atlantic fleet. During October 1963, anti-submarine warfare and ship surveillance were added to the VW-11 mission. By February 1964 all crews were qualified for ASW operations. VW-11 flew the sub barrier and provided a CIC platform for ASW over the north Atlantic until it was decommissioned on October 1, 1965. VW-11 flew its WV-2 aircraft over an estimated 135,000 hours in the worst weather the North Atlantic could throw at its aircraft during its tenure.

VW-12—On July 2, 1956 Airborne Early Warning Squadron VW-12 was commissioned at Naval Air Station Barbers Point, Hawaii. Its mission was to extend the Distant Early Warning line from the Aleutian Island chain to Midway Island. The Pacific Barrier became operational on July 1, 1958. Although VW-12's home port was located at Naval Air Station Barbers point Hawaii, its crews were temporarily assigned to Midway, Island for periods of two weeks at a time and flew the Pacific Barrier from Midway to the Aleutians and back. VW-12 was decommissioned on February 1, 1960. During VW-12's tenure its crews flew over 102,000 hours. Due to difficulty with the provision of personnel, it would be impossible for the Pacific Airborne Early Warning Wing to meet its commitments; VW-12, VW-14, and Airborne Barrier Service Squadron 2 were merged in to Airborne Early Warning Barrier Squadron Pacific on February 1, 1960.

VW-13—On September 1, 1955 Airborne Early Warning Squadron 13 was commissioned at Naval Air Station Patuxent River, Maryland. VW-13 deployed to Argentia, Newfoundland to relieve VW-11 September 1956 and commenced flying the Atlantic Barrier on October 1, 1956. They managed the Atlantic barrier until March 1957 when they were relieved by VW-15. Statistics of the deployment tell the story of Newfoundland weather. The squadron made 410 Ground Control Approaches (GCA). The percentage of instrument landings was 11.2% with a crosswind greater than 25 knots 11.3% of the time. Freezing rain occurred most of the five month period. The average ceiling was 600 feet and the visibility 1½ miles. Twenty-three barrier flights had to go to alternate stations. Turbulence both light and heavy was encountered during 53% of their flights. The winter was cold to the point that during one 10 day stretch the temperature didn't rise above 32 degrees. VW-13 was decommissioned September 15, 1957. The reason for its decommissioning was to reduce the number of AEW squadrons to two. They were VW-11 and VW-15. VW-13 was re-commissioned June 3, 1958. In January 1959 a VW-13 lost an aircraft landing at Argentia during a foggy approach on three engines. All hands were saved with exception of one. The pilot and 2nd pilot were awarded the Navy Cross trying to save the crewman. The plane was a total loss. Although home based at Naval Station Patuxent River, Maryland VW-13 maintained a deployment of crew and aircraft in Argentia, Newfoundland and flew the Atlantic Barrier with its sister squadrons VW-11 and VW15 until June 30, 1961. VW-13 was deployed permanently to Argentia on July 1, 1961. In August VW-13 deployed its crews to Keflavik, Iceland and be come part of Detachment 13 flying a new Greenland-Iceland-Great Britain Barrier.

In March of 1962 VW-13 participated in the U. S. Navy Hydrographic Office's "Project Birdseye". The scientific and tactical objectives of "Birdseye" were to collect information for the development of techniques which would make it possible to predict changes in ice distributions and characteristics. The compilation of this data into an improved ice atlas, and provided the evaluation of aerial observation techniques and of the use of electronic equipment used for determining ice features. VW-13 provided the WV and crew to accomplish this mission. During this two week task the crew worked out of Birdseye's staging areas, Thule Greenland and Eielson, AFB Alaska. VW-13 continued this project until decommissioning. On July 30, 1963 VW-13 lost an aircraft while doing training. The crew and plane were doing touch and goes at Gander, Newfoundland. Although there were minor injuries, no crew was lost. The aircraft was a total loss. During May 1964 one of VW-13's WVs was returned modified for ASW activity. In addition to its barrier mission VW-13 started

ASW and ship surveillance work. This continued until decommissioning on July 30, 1965.

VW-14—On July 1, 1957 Airborne Early Warning Squadron VW-13 was commissioned at Naval Air Station Barbers Point, Hawaii. Its mission was to provide Airborne Early Warning Service in alerting the Continental United States against attacks through the Pacific Ocean Area. Upon the decommissioning of VW-16 on October 1 1957, VW-14 received 45 aviators, 17 officers, and 133 enlisted men from VW-16. On December 23, 1957, a VW-14 WV-2 was ditched in the sea north of the Island of Oahu. There were 4 survivors, with 19 hands lost. On February 1, 1960 VW-14 was dis-established. During its tenure VW-14 flew over 58,000 hours. On February 1, 1960 VW-14 was merged with VW-12 and Airborne Service Squadron 2 to form Airborne Early Warning Squadron Pacific. This was done to enable Airborne Early Warning Wing Pacific to continue meeting its Barrier Pacific commitments.

VW-15—On October of 1955 VW-15 was commissioned at Naval Air Station Patuxent River, Maryland. Although VW-15 was home based at Patuxent River, VW-15 shared flying the Atlantic Barrier with its' sister squadrons VW-11 and VW-13 through its decommissioning. VW-15 was unfortunate during its tenure losing three aircraft. One aircraft was lost following a hard landing in Argentia Newfoundland during a crosswind landing. The aircraft was a total loss. One aircraft crashed off the end of the runway at Argentia during a Ground Control Approach. 11 crewmen were lost. The final aircraft lost disappeared at the end of the Atlantic Barrier over the ocean. No wreckage was ever found. 22 crewmen were lost. VW-15 was decommissioned in June, 1961

VW-16—was established at Naval Air Station Barbers Point, Hawaii on July 1, 1957. VW-16 and was decommissioned on October 1, 1957. This was done due to limited personnel becoming available to man crews for three Airborne Early Warning Squadrons at Barbers Point. During its tenure VW-16 flew 2200 hours of training time.

Appendix 3

Flight Engineers Lament

We have many problems can't you see,
So I'll spin a tale of misery.
You are not the Chaplin that is true,
But this sad tale I'll tell to you.

We are on the West end of DEW,
They call us A-E-Double you.
We fly the Willy Victor plane,
And we've driven Barsron quite insane.

We wonder where the B-MEPS went,
When the fuel leaked past the vapor vent.
And while you're watching for a warning light,
The R-P-M drifts out of sight.

We engineers did check the craft,
But you know all engineers are daft.
But everything's all right we know,
By the way the analyzers glow.

The planes just sit out on the line,
They're out of commission most of the time.
The NC-5 just sits and jerks,
Until you call public works.

We sit at barigold for one hour,
The radars looking awful sour.
The P.C. looks out to port,
Perhaps we're scheduled to abort.

The 2P has forgotten his pipe,
Right away a downing gripe.
The cooling caps all seen to tight,
We just don't want to fly tonight.

And now we're off into the blue,
All those dials are in horrible view.
While our friends are drinking beer,
We have to spend the night up here.

We will return to earth with zest,
Thinking of a day of rest.
But at Barsron we'll take some swipes,
And write a page of petty gripes.

Appendix 4

The Main Bases
Argentia Newfoundland

Naval Station Argentia was established under the British United States lend lease program and was first occupied on January 25, 1941. Occupation followed the expropriation of the flat land formed by a small bay called Little Placentia Sound and the Western end facing Placentia Bay by the Newfoundland Government. Newfoundland at that time was the Dominion of Newfoundland. It became the 10th province of Canada in the year of 1949. Over 400 families were displaced to enable the development of the Naval Station and its associated Air Station. Construction crews were rushed to build the base and its adjoining airfield. On July 15, 1941 the base was officially commissioned.

The locations first claim to fame began on August 7, 1941. Then President Roosevelt arrived on the USS Augusta which anchored in Placentia Bay. He was awaiting the arrival of Prime Minister Churchill of Great Britain. The British Warship HMS Prince of Wales carrying the Prime Minister arrived August 9, 1941 and anchored close by, also in Placentia Bay. During the anchorage from August 9-12, 1941 President Roosevelt, Prime Minister Churchill and their staffs met to discuss war strategies and logistics once the United States joined the war. They also negotiated a press release they called a "joint statement." The conference concluded the evening of August 12, 1941. Following a formal passing of review of British and United States ships both leaders ships left for home. The press statement was issued on August 14, 1941 simultaneously in Washington DC and London, England. Several days later the London Herald characterized the statement as being the Atlantic Charter. There never was a signed (by either part) legal document called the "Atlantic Charter."

On August 28, 1941 Naval Air Station Argentia was commissioned NAS Argentia. It was built on a plateau atop the triangular peninsula adjacent to Naval Stations anchorage and shore facilities. Initially the Naval Air Station was used for base convoy protection, coastal patrols, and anti submarine aircraft. Both land based aircraft and seaplanes were used for these purposes. Although both commands were separate both were viewed as one.

The history of Argentia continues as the USS Prairie is stationed at Argentia during summer 1941 and serves as CTF-24 Flag Headquarters. In February

1942, Argentia became the center of one of the worst disasters in the US Navy's history. The ships USS Pollux and the USS Trustun were wrecked 75 miles southwest of the base. Over 100 victims are buried in Argentia's military cemetery.

March 1942 brought the US Army to Argentia. They established Ft. McAndrew to provide security to the navy base. The Army built an anti aircraft battery at that location. Later that year Britain's Royal Navy established a small maintenance base to service its ships involved in convoy escort groups operating out of Halifax, Sydney, Nova Scotia and In the Gulf of St. Lawrence. In the spring of 1942 a 7000 ton dry dock was installed along with a ship repair facility. In August 1943 CTF-24 Flag Headquarters moved ashore to permanent facilities.

In 1944 Argentia was used as one of two stop over bases for refueling, maintenance, and crew changes for the 6 Navy K-ships (blimps) that made the first transatlantic crossings of Blimps K-23 Nd K-130 from blimp Squadron 14 that left Massachusetts on May 28, 1944 and landed at Argentia approx. 16 hours later. The next four blimps followed the first two on June 11 and 27, 1944. Their initial mission was to conduct nighttime anti-submarine operations to complement the FAW-15 Aircraft (PBY's and B24s). They also did mine spotting and anti-submarine patrols in the Rock of Gibraltar area.

Following the end of the War during August, 1945, the first dependants of naval personnel moved to Argentia in permanent housing. The following year Fort McAndrew was transferred to the United States Army Air Force (USAAF). In 1947, the USAAF became the United States Air Force (USAF) and Ft. McAndrews became McAndrew Air Force Base. Argentia became a key "node" on the Northwest Atlantic SOSUS network used to track Soviet Nuclear Submarines. The base was the target of several espionage attempts between the late1940's and 1990's as a result.

In 1955 McAndrew AFB was decommissioned and the facility was turned over to the Navy. It was in July of 1955 that Atlantic Airborne Early Warning Wing was commissioned. The first Squadron of the Wing VW-11 was commissioned in August 1, 1955 with VW-13 and VW-15 commissioned in following months. VW-11 was scheduled to fly the first barrier from Argentia, Newfoundland in 10 months following its commissioning. The Commanding Officer of Naval Station Argentia and liaison personnel for the Early Warning Wing worked diligently together on house keeping quarters and supply facilities. Flight communications, airfield status, quarters for personnel, and recreational facilities were determined and construction work commenced. Continuous progress checks were made on the construction of the new Miami hanger and the new BOQ. The new BOQ was named the Argentia Hilton. It had the distinction of being the tallest building in Newfoundland until the Newfoundlanders destroyed it in 1967. Activity was accelerated and buildings and equipment were being built all over the base. The date for completion was 1 May 1956 when VW-11 was scheduled for its first duty in Argentia. Over 600 men and their WV-2 aircraft were scheduled to begin arriving to fly the first barriers. This would be the largest Navy squadron to move at one time in Navy history. The effort at Argentia was successful and completed on time.

Argentia Naval Base was the home of a number Air Commands.:

COMAEWINGLANT—Responsible for conducting airborne early warning operations as directed. Manage logistics and type command within command.

COMFAIRARGENTIA—Responsible for necessary administrative co-ordination and material support of all U. S. Navy aviation units inn the Newfoundland area.

COMBARLFORANT—Responsible for operational control of all air, surface and sub-surface units engaged in operations and fleet exercises along the Greenland, Iceland, United Kingdom Line, and the Atlantic AEW/ASW barrier through task force commanders.

COMBARGENTIA—Responsible for operational control over all air and surface units manning the Argentia AEW/ASW barrier.

COMARGENTIAPATGRU—Responsible for operational control over U. S. Navy ASW patrol aircraft units assigned to operate from Argentia.

COMRICEREC & ICEFCSTGRU—Responsible for operational control over aircraft units and aero logical units which provide information necessary to support MSTS shipping in the Arctic regions of the Atlantic.

In addition to Air Early Warning Squadrons flying from Argentia, various ASW patrol squadrons and Ice patrol squadrons flew out of Argentia Naval Air Station.

The barriers were flown from Argentia on a 7 day per week 365 day basis by VW-11, VW-13, and VW-15 on a rotational basis until April of 1958 when

VW-11 was ordered to permanently move to Argentia. Prior to that timeframe Argentia began again prepping for an influx of new personnel. That is, dependants of VW-11 personnel. Both officer and enlisted men quarters had to be built and furnished. The logistics of moving hundreds of wives and children had to be managed and accommodated by Naval Station Argentia. The needs of housewives, mothers and children had to be met and in a location that was not like home in the United States. Quite a job, but it was accomplished, not without issues, but was completed.

On July 1, 1965, VW-11 became the last operational barrier squadron and maintained the barrier for two months by itself. The last barrier was flown out of Argentia on August 26, 1965. On October 7, 1965, the North Atlantic extension of the Distant Early Warning (DEW) was officially ended. VW-11 was decommissioned. The WV-2 aircraft were flown to Davis Moncton AFB in Arizona for their final resting place. The aircraft took its place in naval history. It was one that flew thousands of hours safely and completed its mission successfully.

Argentia Naval Station was decommissioned in 1973. The land was transferred to Canada in 1975. The last Navy personnel moved out in 1994 closing a very successful chapter in Navy History. It was a base that many sailors spent some of their careers at and were happy to leave. It was a place where many families lived and raised their children. It was a location that served the North American continent admirably. Its personnel and equipment protected the United States and Canada and the free world from the Soviet Union without question and did it with diligence and personal commitment. They gave their lives and souls for their nation. They even had some fun doing it.

NAS Barbers Point

Hawaii

Barbers Point was named for Henry Barber, master of the Arthur, a 100 foot British brigantine that ran aground on the point of Oahu during a storm in 1796. Captain Henry Barber was determined to get underway despite the storm and hoisted anchor on his hundred foot brig on October 31, 1796. All other captains kept their vessels in port while the Arthur was deluged by wind, rain, and pounding surf. The ship went down taking with it all but 6 crew members and its captain. The survivors came ashore near a tract of land referred to by native Hawaiians as Kalaeloa, a legendary birthplace of Hawaiian Kings. Kalaeloa later became known as Barbers Point.

In the early 1930s the Navy leased a 3000 square foot piece of land from the estate of James Campbell. This tract was to be used as a mooring post for the dirigible, Akron. Later in the 1930s the Navy leased another section of land from the estate and built a 1500 foot outlying field near the mooring post for Navy dirigibles, none of which ever cruised by Hawaii. In September 1940 when the lease expired, the Navy acquired an additional 3500 acres from the Campbell estate for the enlargement of the outlying field which became Marine Corps Air Station Ewa. The site was chosen as an ideal peace time air training station and was completed early in 1941. With the ground breaking, plans were already being developed for an expansion of naval aviation facilities at Barbers Point. The construction of an airfield west of Ewa began in November 1941, but was temporarily suspended after the Japanese attack on Pearl Harbor. Construction began again shortly after the attack so that the field could be completed quickly thereafter. The Ewa Marine Corps Air station sustained a large amount of damage. Nine of eleven Wildcats, 19 of 32 scout bombers, and six utility aircraft were totally destroyed. Barbers Point, originally intended as an out lying field for Naval Air Station Ford Island was still not completed when it was established as a naval air station on 15 August 1942 with 14 officers and 242 enlisted personnel. The new Air Station became a hub of aviation as the Navy used it to carry the war across the Pacific. By the end of World War II the Naval Air Station was home to almost 13,000 personnel. Following the end of the war Naval Air Station Barbers became a rapid demobilization center.

During the late 1940's Naval Air Station Barbers Point became the beneficiary of a consolidation of Naval facilities on the leeward side of the island Oahu. It absorbed Marine Corps Air Station Ewa in 1952 and Coast Guard aircraft at Kaneohe were moved to Barbers Point. When the war in Korea began in 1951, Naval Air Station Barbers Point became a critical staging for supplies, equipment and forward deploying squadrons. New construction included weapons and jet engine testing facilities, a survival equipment shop and more than a thousand housing sites. Naval Air Station Barber Points became one of the most modern Patrol Squadron homeports in the world.

During the Korean war and the cold war Naval Air Station Barbers Point was most famous for its Rainbow fleet. Its VP squadrons deployed P2Vs and P3Vs to patrol the Pacific, and supported the Korean and the Viet Nam Wars. In 1956 Airborne Early Warning Squadron Two transferred to NAS Barber Point to extend the DEW line across the Pacific. The WV2 Super Constellations operated by VW-12 and VW-14 maintained a continuous barrier over the Pacific until 1965. The two squadrons were merged in 1960 to form the Airborne Early Warning Squadron Pacific.

During the 1960's NAS Barbers Point provided support to operations in Viet Nam while concurrently supporting the patrol communities training and operational readiness. In addition to its patrol squadron operations, NAS Barbers Point hosted a continuously changing group of various fleet supporting squadrons such as anti-submarine helicopter groups.

The end of the cold war in which Barbers Point was such an important factor eventually brought about its closure. In 1993, Congress accepted the recommendation of the Base Realignment and Closure Commission (BRAC) that NAS Barbers Point be closed. The Coast Guard remained at Barbers Point and the Navy retained 1100 acres for military housing and family support facilities. The remainder of the 2150 acres were ceded to Hawaii. For more than a half of a century the Naval Air Station had been the pride of the Pacific. It was the home of the Rainbow fleet. The closure of Naval Air Station Barbers Point is the final chapter in its distinguished history. Hence, the finest Naval Air Station in the Western Hemisphere was closed.

Appendix 5

In Memory of
The Will Victor Roster

The Losses, Men and Machines

December 9, 1954

Squadron: Naval Air Developmental Unit
Aircraft: WV-2 131387
Location: Naval Air Facility Johnsville , Pennsylvania
Loss of life: None

September 17, 1956

Squadron: AEWRON 3 (VW-3)
Aircraft: WV-3 137393
Location: 100 miles south of Guam
Loss of life: None, all hands rescued.

April 17, 1957

Squadron: AEWRON 15 (VW-15)
Aircraft: WV-2 141314
Location: Naval Air Stations Argentia, Newfoundland
Loss of life: None, only injury among 24 man crew was a sprained ankle.

October 7, 1957

Squadron: AEWRON 4 (VW-4)
Aircraft: WV-3 137897
Location: Naval Air Station Jacksonville, Florida
Loss of life: None. Crew abandoned aircraft safely.

December 23, 1957

Squadron: AIRBARSRON-2, mission flown by VW-14 crew 20
Aircraft WV-2 143197
Location: 25 miles northwest of the Island of Oahu
Loss of life: 4 crew were rescued. 19 lives were lost

Members of crew lost:

CDR Fred Woodward
ENS Lewis Webb
ENS Douglas E. Roberts
Douglas D. Cellam, AE2
Robert O. Clark, ACW3
Shearl L. Cook, AT1
Harold O. Dodd, ACWAN
Francis Maltby, AN
Mark M. McBride, AN
Henry Murdaugh, AD1
Robert H. Neil, AD1
Michael A. Pietruciolli, AN
Clarence W. Polson, AT3
Charles Price, ACW3, VW-12
Daniel D. Raymond, ACW3
William E. Richards, AL1
James Rush, AT3
Charles E. Slay, AN
Robert Staff, AD1

January 14, 1958

Squadron: AEWRON 11 (VW-11)
Aircraft: R7V-1 128437
Location: Naval Air Station Patuxent River, Maryland
Loss of life: 9 crew were lost.

Members of crew lost:

CDR William W. Lamar Jr.
CDR Richard H. Hart
LTJG Harry G. Morgan Jr.
Vito Paulauskas, ACW2
Edward R. Liberda, ACW1
Larry W. Rudder, AT3
William C. Thurau, AE3
Zane H. Krenke, AMM1
Floyd O. Taylor, AMM1

February 20, 1958

Squadron: AEWRON 15 (VW-15)
Aircraft: WV-2 141310
Location: 110 miles West of Corvo Island, Azores

This writer was flying for VW-11 four hours behind this aircraft and tried vainly to contact the aircraft via radio with out results.

Loss of life: 22 crew were lost, all presumed dead.

Crew members lost:
CDR Earl P. McBride
LCDR Peter F. Lorah
LT Paul L. Brousseau
LTJG Don Y Engell Jr.
LTJG Alan R. Gray
LTJG James W. Levans
Charles P. Barthholomew, AE2
Lewis B. Brantly, AN
Paul R. Durrance, AN
Johnnie R. Forester, AT1
Floyd George, AMM1
Stanley A. Gillette, AN
William J. Graham, ACW2
Robert J. Harris, ATC
Jerry L. Hollingsworth, ACW3
Donald R. Jacobson, ACW2
Melvin D. Knighton, AT3
William J Martinez, AMM1
Jimmie D. McIntosh, ACW3
Dale L. Shober, AT3
Donald D. Stevenson, AT2

October 18, 1958

Squadron: AEWRON 15 (VW-15)
Aircraft: WV-2 141294
Location: Naval Air Station Argentia, Newfoundland

Loss of life: 19 crew rescued, 11 crew lost their lives.

Crew members lost:

CDR Raymond L. Klassy, VW-13
LT Donald A. Becker
ENS Donald E. Mulligan
A. S. Corrado
Robert N. Elliot, AN
R. J Emerson
Clarence J. Shea
J. E. Strange
D.D. Wilson
Lyle W. Foster, American Red Cross
William Serome Taylor, AD3, Body never recovered

March 29, 1959 (Easter Sunday)

Squadron: AWERON 15 (VW-15)
Aircraft: WV- 2 141332
Location: Naval Air Station Argentia, Newfoundland

Loss of life: All crew members escaped. There were no injuries to the 21 crew members.

April 2, 1959

Squadron: AEWRON 13 (VW-13)
Aircraft: WV-2 141303
Location: Naval Air Station Argentia, Newfoundland

Loss of life: 28 crew members escaped and were uninjured. 1 crew member was lost.

LT Day the planes pilot was awarded the Navy and Marine Corps Medal for climbing back in aircraft to rescue crew.

Crew members lost:

William N Brenner AT1

October 31, 1960

Squadron: OCEANOGRAPHIC DEVELOPMENT SQUADRON 8 (VXN-8)
Aircraft: WV-2 126513
Location: McMurdo Sound, Antarctica

Loss of life: There were no fatalities. 8 personnel were injured of 23 crew and passengers

January 22, 1961

Squadron: AEWBARRONPAC
Aircraft: WV-2 143193
Location: Naval Air Station Midway Island, TH
Loss of life: 6 of 23 crew members and 3 of 3 crash crew perished.

Crew members lost:

LTJG E. Mills
Robert J. Baxter, AT3
James E. Koehn, ACW2
William R. Long, AT3
David B. Turner, AT3
Jan J. Waddingham, ACW3

Crash Crew members lost:

Ronald E. Blakeman, AM3
Gordon G. Blatchley, AB3
Robert J. Razey, AN

February, 1962

Squadron: AEWRON 4 (VW-4)
Aircraft: WV-3 141323
Location: Naval Station Roosevelt Roads, Puerto Rico

Loss of life: None

May 22, 1962

Squadron: FLEET AIRBORNE REONNAISSANCE SQUADRON 2 (VQ-2)
Aircraft: WV-2Q 131390
Location: 1-1/4 mile SW of Markt Schwaben, Germany

Loss of life: All of 26 members of crew lost.

Crew members lost:

LCDR Conner M. Petrie Jr.
LCDR Charles A. Patschke
LTJG Robert Poole
Gilbert J. Austin,ATRAN
Donald R. Ballard, AT2
Gene P. Bartram, AT1
Martin J. Brennan, AM1
Gerald R. Carlton, AT2
Eugeno George, ADRCA
Edward N. Hawkins, ATR3
Gerhard K Heimerl, AMH1
Michael Kostiuk, ADR2
Orville R. Malone, ATS3
Jared M. Rose, ATCA
Timothy D. Steward, AE3
Lee P. Strong, ATN3
Jamos W. Tyler AT2
Ronald P Wajda, AT2
Joesph H. Watkins, ATR3
Thomas E. Young, ATCA
F. L. Breshmars, SP5, US Army
R. J. Hoos, SP5, US Army
R. A. Lewis, SP5, US Army
E. M. McGreal, SP5, US Army

August 9, 1962

Squadron: AEWRON TRAINING UNIT ATLANTIC (AEWTULANT)
Aircraft: WV-2 141324
Location: Naval Air Station Patuxent River, Maryland
Loss of life: 14 crew members escaped. 5 crew members lost.

Crew members lost:

LCDR Wallace Irvin Anderson
LT Walter Russell Filmore
John Mark Heinbach, AMMCM
Dale Lloyd Peyton, AT2
Kenneth Willoughby Taylor, ACW3

July, 31, 1963

Squadron: AEWRON 13 (VW-13)
Aircraft: WV-2 141329
Location: Gander Airbase, Newfoundland

Loss of life: None of crew was lost. Two crew members of 7 were injured.

August 23, 1964

Squadron: AEWRON 4 (VW-4)
Aircraft: WV-3 137891
Location: Hurricane Cleo, Approximately 100 miles south /southwest of
Puerto Rico

Loss of life: There was no loss of life. There were many crew members severely
injured.

June 11, 1965

Squadron: AEWRON 13 (VW-13)
Aircraft: WV-2 141321
Location: Naval Air Station Keflavik, Iceland
Loss of life: one ground crew member was trapped and crushed inside wheel well.

Ground crew member lost:

Michael Andriolla, AD3

August 20, 1965

Squadron: FLEET AIEBORNE RECONNAISSANCE SQADRON 1 (VQ-1)
Aircraft: WV-2M (EC121M)
Location: Naval Air Station Atsugi, Japan

Loss of life: No crew members were lost. One crew member was injured

April 14, 1969

Squadron: FLEET AIRBORNE RECONNAISSANCE SQUADRON 1
(VQ-1)
Aircraft: WV-2 (EC121M)
Location: South East of Chongjin, Korea

Loss of life: 31 of 31 crew members were lost.

Crew members lost:

LCDR James H. Overstreet
LT John N. Dzema
LT Dennis B. Gleason
LT Peter P Perrottet
LT John H. Singer
LT Robert F. Taylor
LTJG Joseph R. Ribar
LTJG Robert Y. Sykora
LTJG Norman E. Wilkerson
Louis F. Balderman, ADR2
Stephan F. Chartier, AT1
Bernie J. Colgin, AT1
Ballard F. Conners Jr. ,ADR1
Gary R. DuCharme, CT3
Gene K. Graham, ATN3
LaVerne A. Greiner, AEC
Dennis J. Horrigan, ATR2
Richard H. Kincaid, ATN2
Marshall M. McNamara, ADRC
Timothy H. McNeil, ATR3
John A. Miller, CT3
John H. Potts, CT1
Richard T. Prindle, AMS3
Fredrick A. Randall, CTC
James Leroy Roach, AT1
Richard E. Smith, CTC
Phillip D. Sundby, CT3
Richard E. Sweeney, AT1
Stephen J. Tesmer, CT2
David M. Willis, ATN3
Hugh M. Lynch, SSGT, United States Marines

March 16, 1970

Squadron: FLEET AIRBORNE RECONNAISSANCE SQUADRON 1
(VQ-1)
Aircraft: WV-2 145927
Location: DaNang, AO, Republic Viet Nam

Loss of life: 24 of 31 crew member were lost. 6 of 7 crew members were
gravely injured.

Crew members lost:

LCDR Harvey C.K. Aiua
LCDR Harry C. Martin
LT George L. Morningstar
LT Robin A. Pearce
LTJG James M. Masters Jr.
LTJG George E. Pressler
LTJG Jean P. Souzon
William John Risse, ADRC
Larry O. Marchbank, AT1
Arthur D. Simmons, ADR1
Donald W. Wilson, ADR1
Floyd E. Andrus III, AE2
Gregory J. Ashbeck, ADR3
William P. Bletsh, AMS2
Guy Thomas Denton, ATN2
Joseph S. Saukaitis, ATR2
John S. Schaefer, ATN2
Stuart J. Scruggs, ADR2
Barry M. Searby, ATN2
John Macy Birch, ATN3
Thurle E, Case Jr., ATN3
Ben Allen Hughes, ATN3
Ralph S. Purhum, ATN3

Aircraft status: Only two Willy Victors returned to normal flying status. One
other aircraft never flew correctly again.

Bibliography

Dewline Chronicles-A history by Lynden T. (Bucky Harris) Harris

The Queen of the Skies-Claude G. Luisada

The Keel—The Story initial training in the United States Navy—Albert Love
Enterprises

VW-1 History—Jim Galinsky, George Stewart, Pete Wasmund, Dan Ragan
William D'Aoust, Charles E. Lange, Gary Oulman

Coast Guard Air Station Barbers Point/Naval Air Station Barbers Point—global
security. org/military/facility/barbers-point.htm—maintained by John Pike

The Engineers Lament—An anonymous Flight Engineer—BARSRON

The Willy Victor Roster—http://personal.riverusers.com/-elmccaul/MEMORIAM.
htm

Wikopedia.org/wiki/Naval-Air-Station-Patuxent-River

Willy Victor.COM—maintained by Jack Web

Naval Aviation Archives—Navy Yard-Washington DC

About the Author

How did I get involved in the cold war. Let me begin when we moved into my mother's dream house. It began in the summer of 1949 when we moved into our new house in Garfield Heights, Ohio, a suburb of Cleveland, Ohio. It is a blue collar town made up of people of mixed heritages. The population was made up of many different ethnic groups: Polish, Italians, German, Hungarians, Slovenians, Irish, and people of dark complexion all living in peace and harmony with common goals. Garfield Heights was just like many towns and cities across the United States of America. These were people that worked hard, where dads worked at factory jobs and got paid on Fridays. After work on Friday they went to the bar to drink with the boys and in many cases came home drunk. Most parents and grandparents had been through the stock market crash of 1929 and had lost much of what they had worked for up till then and were very conservative with their money. Banks were still suspicious and I'm sure some money was still kept under many mattresses. Most parents wanted to raise their kids to have a better life and education than they had and wanted them to be more successful than they were. College was a dream for their kids, but they wanted their kids to attend if at all possible. They taught their kids to work hard and believed that with hard work they would achieve success. The American dream was for all who were willing to work for it. Garfield Heights was a bedroom community. That is mostly homes, with very little business other than a few delicatessens or local butchers. There were no shopping centers until 1954. The new shopping center on Turney road was started in late 1954. It was a good place for a kid to grow up. The people were a mix of good Christian folks who worked hard and instilled a strong work ethic in their children. Most moms stayed home to raise the kids. Their homes were called bungalows and had two bedrooms, a bath, living room, kitchen with eating space and a basement. In the attic of many homes, two additional bedrooms were added. They were great starter homes for young couples with small children and a step up from rent.

Most folks either served in or had relatives who served in World War II. These were either folks who immigrated to the USA from around the world during the early 1900's or first generation born Americans trying to achieve the American dream for their families. These were people who were proud to be citizens of the USA and respected the stars and stripes. It was a town where the Cub Scouts, Brownies, Bluebirds, Girl Scouts, and Boy Scouts thrived. Where you were a kid and a member of these groups and it was mandatory to learn the National Anthem and America the Beautiful. Memorial Day and the Fourth of July were special patriotic days in Garfield Heights. Parades and picnics for all who wished to participate—Flags, ribbons, bands, and the Red, White and Blue. Military personnel, Veterans of Foreign Wars, the American Legion were highly respected special groups of participants. World War II was still in the minds of the adults. Ike was President and life was mostly good for all. Veterans of the War were heroes. This was a town that although very unique in its own way, yet resembled many towns or small cities across the USA.

My parents were victims of the depression who lost their life savings and worked hard to buy the house in Garfield Heights in 1949. During the War my dad was too old to be drafted but, volunteered like many others to be an Auxiliary policeman and fireman. He also was in the Coast Guard Auxiliary. He was proud of his efforts. So was I. He and mom worked hard to get what they achieved. My mom stayed at home taking care of my sister and me until she decided that we needed things in the house. She went to work for the Bell System as a telephone operator.

Garfield Heights was a perfect location for my sister and me. The neighborhood was full of kids to play with. There was a large park down the street for us to explore and a safe city to grow up in. I remember that doors of most homes weren't locked and windows were open in the summer. People trusted each other in those days. The house in Garfield Heights was sort of my mom's dream house. She helped the builder design it. I started at Garfield Heights elementary school in the 5th grade. I was a little guy, a little apprehensive on the first day, but got through the initial apprehension of not knowing anyone in my class. We were told we were the future of the Country. How naive we were. We were living in what the press called a Cold War that most of us knew nothing about. The North Koreans invaded South Korea and the United States was sending troops to help repel the invaders. Just a skirmish we were told. The draft was still being used and 18 year olds were still going into the service to participate in this skirmish. Many of them lost their lives in a forbidding place far from home. For us kids it was a great time to be growing up. Just kids, doing what kids do.

World War II was over, we thought the world was again safe, most folks were working, the economy was booming. I contracted double pneumonia that winter and almost died. Thanks to the development of sulfa drugs during the war and Dr. Joe I survived. Dr. Joe was a special person dad said. Dad apparently had known him as a kid and helped him in someway to get to become a Doctor. I never ever knew what dad did to help him.

I started playing the trumpet in the 5th grade and joined the band that year. As she always did, mom wanted the best for me when she bought my first trumpet and started my first lessons. I took lessons from a man who played in the Cleveland symphony and he sold her the same type of trumpet he played. I became rather proficient as a trumpet player over the years. The first two years in elementary school went rather quickly. I was a young boy, school and play was fun. The summer after the 6th grade television began to be introduced. Some of our neighbors had TVs as they were known and we were invited to watch with them. Wow, what an invention! You could now see what you were hearing on the radio. It was amazing. Just before I started school that fall dad and mom bought a 12 inch Television set. It took two men to deliver it and set up the antenna. "Dog Ears" they were called. We were in our glory. The wood color of the set didn't match the rest of the furniture in the house, the color was blond, the rest was maple. When mom asked dad "Why didn't you get a Maple colored one?" Dad shrugged his shoulders and replied weakly, "They didn't have one. This was the only color they had and the price was right, so I bought it." I was happy he bought it, no matter what color it was. We watched it a lot. Saturday night was special as my sister and I got to stay up past our normal bedtime and watch Uncle Milty. My sister and I did what most kids did every day, go outside and play all day. Mom would have to call us for lunch and dinner. What fun we had, parents did not worry about perverts or bad people picking on kids. In our neighborhood there were kids on the street all the time. We watched out for strangers and each other.

I made it through the 5th and 6th grades without any difficulty and graduated to the big high school for the 7th grade. We were the class of 1956. How proud we were. We were going to make a difference at Garfield Heights High School (GHHS). Our class was the largest class in the school as 7th graders and would be the largest class to graduate in 1956 since the school opened in 1932. GHHS was the first million dollar high school to be built in the USA.

I can't imagine how the people in Garfield Heights felt when the school opened. How excited they must have been. What a difference between the old school and this one. We had our own lockers for our stuff. We had to change classes every hour or so. We had to eat in the cafeteria or walk home for lunch. The school was big. Three floors tall and the halls were filled with people during the period changes. The 11th and 12th graders were so big compared to us peanuts. We had to run to classes to keep up. All new people again. We all were changing over from kids to teenagers. We were going through something called puberty. Some of us were getting to wherever we were going faster than others. Boys' voices were getting deeper and getting hair between their legs.

Girls were getting breasts. What differences. I don't think puberty hit me until later. Maybe the 9th grade. But, that didn't make much difference as I had my favorite girls. I liked them more than others. I had no idea why. We even had "Sock Hops" after school to meet new people and dance. No sock hops for me even though the girls tried to talk us guys into attending. The older girls were built like my mother. Isn't that interesting? During my introduction to the big school I met five friends that would last a lifetime. There was David Zyzock, Tom Seese, Pat, (Pasqulino, Lino) Mastro, Bob Watch, and Don Snitske. What a group we made. We shared the same things. Backgrounds the same and needs the same, we traveled together, partied together and shared many of the same experiences together. We shared our secrets and supported each other as life as teenagers went forward. We could have been called a gang as we bought the same jackets and hung around with each other. We were just a group of guys who were great friends and still remain that way today.

In the early 50's "Rock and Roll" was beginning to bloom and growing at a rapid rate. "Moon Dog" Alan Freid and his friends were rocking and rolling on the radio and television. Disk Jockeys were the rage. In Cleveland it was Bill Randle, Phil McClain, and Joe Finan. Elvis Presley hit the country like a bomb. One of my buddies, Bob Watch's, Dad was the engineer for Joe Finan. Finan was a Disc Jockey for local radio station WJW. His dad brought records home for Bob and me to listen to and make recommendations for Finan to play. We were the experts. I'm sure we must have listened to hundreds of records at Bob's house. Finan listened to us and played our recommended songs. At least we heard them on his show.

Snooky Lansen and friends had a popular song program on Saturday nights for us teens. At many parties on Saturday night the necking stopped for the "Hit Parade' on television. High school made a large impact on me. It was life changing. Sports were the favorite thing for me. I had played sports from the time I was in the eighth grade until I graduated from high school. I participated in baseball, basketball, track, and football. Football was the favorite sport. I played trumpet in the band and moved on to the French horn during the 11th grade. I guess I just wanted a change. High school was something that was not a challenge but, something to enjoy and participate in. I was very involved with sports, band, acting, school dances, people, teachers, and all things related. One of the best things that happens to a boy as he is growing up is the awakening to the finer points of girls. Education was important and I did learn a lot. I found out what girls were all about. At least I thought I knew. They, the girls taught me a lot about what made them tick and how to treat them. The boys agreed that there was nothing like girls breasts' and their pubic hair. These things were important to me. Although one did not get to touch much of either one. The girls would have belted you. Necking was in, but touching was out. Our girls wore wool skirts down to their ankles in the winter and wide skirts with layers of crinoline slips under them in the summer. No matter how hard you tried for a beaver shot or a touch, there just weren't any. If you were going steady with a girl maybe there might be an opportunity.

During the 11th grade my Uncle Charlie, dad's brother, asked me if I wanted to attend one of the military academies for my college education. I said, "No, who wants to be in the military?" I think Uncle Charlie was trying to help, but I was committed to a different direction. Dad never said a word. What an interesting question at the time I thought. But, I was enjoying myself, confident that I was going to graduate, go to college, and become a football coach. Football was my game. I loved it. Coaching was my dream. I wanted to coach football. My hero was Coach Ralph Jankowski. He came to Garfield Heights High School during my freshman year. In my eyes he was just awesome person. The girls thought he was handsome. The guys saw him as a rugged tough coach. He was going to make us football players. He came to be known as Ralph to us players. I learned what the game was all about from him. I was a soaking wet 135lbs. linebacker with more guts than brains. I loved the contact, the comradeship and the thrill of victory. The game and Coaching was for me. I had a great sophomore year. I was one of three sophomores to make the varsity team that year. I not only dressed for the varsity games, I also played at the Jr. Varsity level.

After the year was completed, Coach Ralph advised me that Mt. Union College would be seriously looking at me for the next two years. If I stayed healthy I would have an opportunity to possibly be offered a scholarship and play for them. What motivation that gave me. How my self confidence grew. How disappointed I was when during summer practice my junior year. I was clipped from behind and my left knee anterior cruciate ligament was torn. What a disappointment! My junior year season was gone, and although I tried to play during my senior year, the knee didn't hold up. During January of my senior year, I had my knee operated on. It healed well enough to participate on the track team. But, my determination to become a football coach remained.

I started dating a special girl during my junior year. Her name was Sam. We had great times during my junior and senior year. During our senior prom, I took Sam aside and proposed marriage. I don't know what it was that evening, but I said the words and much to my surprise she accepted. We had a great summer planning my coaching career and our future. During early August college was nearing, I visited Ohio University and scheduled my freshman year classes. I knew what my freshman year criteria was going to be and where I would be living in the fall. I was excited and looking forward to the fall. My best bud Tom Seese was also going to attend Ohio University and we would be roommates. I also found out that Marie Eastlick and Joan Beach would also be attending, the same school. I had fallen in kid love with Joan in the 5th grade. Wow, it would be a great time. If I had known what would take place that summer, my life may have changed differently. As it turned out, Sam and I never married.

I met my wife Mary two years after I was mustered out of the Navy. We were married in 1962. We had 3 wonderful children; Michelle, John, and Anthony. We have five grandchildren; Megan, Makenzie, Jacob, Maryn, Kayden, and one great grand son Kale. I had a wonderful career in Telecommunications working for AT&T and the Department of Defense. We moved fourteen times during our marriage and finally retired to North Carolina in September of 2002. I lost my beloved Mary in 2011 after 49 wonderful years of love, appreciation, friendship, and joy. I have been very fortunate in life and am going forward. As a Frenchman said one time "C'est la Vie."